# Only
# Connect

"Live in fragments no longer. Only connect."
E. M. Forster, *Howards End*

# This book belongs to:

Businesses who want to use the ancient power of storytelling to help them better connect and communicate.

# Only Connect

*The Art of Corporate Storytelling*

Robert Mighall

LONDON   MADRID
NEW YORK   MEXICO CITY
BARCELONA   MONTERREY

Published by
LID Publishing Ltd
6-8 Underwood Street
London N1 7JQ
United Kingdom
info@lidpublishing.com

A member of:

www.businesspublishersroundtable.com

Printed in Great Britain by TJ International Ltd

ISBN: 978-1-907794-45-2
Cover design: Jevon Downer and Nicholas May
Page design: Nicholas May and Damian Nowell

*For Mr Carl Radley.*
*Where the Story begins.*

# Contents

---

# *The End?*

# preface:
# A Tale of Two CVs

—

I'll start by sharing my own story. Or, rather, 'stories'.

For some years now I've maintained two CVs. The first tells how I was once a fellow in English Literature at an Oxford College, and then the editor of the Penguin Classics series. It lists the books I have written, including an academic study of Victorian Gothic fiction (of interest to about 100 people on the planet); a biography of the Romantic poet John Keats; and my introductions to works by the likes of Oscar Wilde and William Shakespeare. There's also a cultural history of sunshine I wrote about an obsession of mine. But like everything on this CV, it has nothing to do with how I earn my living. Which is why I need a second CV.

After Penguin, I stumbled into corporate branding, where I have worked ever since. An old friend needed some extra brainpower for a naming project his agency was working on. "You're good at words", he reasoned, "and it's words we need urgently". So I gave it a bash, spun out a long list, and the agency liked what I did. So much, that they offered me a job as a consultant. I told them I knew very little about branding, and even less about the world of business it was there to brand. But they saw potential and took a chance. And so, here I am many years later, with a second CV telling a very different story.

My two CVs reflect a broader divide in Anglo-American society, where there simmers a mutual suspicion, even hostility, between art and commerce, high culture and high finance. This division goes back at least to the Victorian age, when the new captains of industry consciously rejected the effete, dying world of the aristocracy. Many were religious non-conformists, which meant they were excluded from Oxbridge, which only admitted Anglicans, and where the study of Greek and Roman classics was considered an essential part of a gentleman's education. When the poet Matthew Arnold's *Culture and Anarchy* (1869) coined the term 'Philistines' to characterise these industrialists' indifference to culture in pursuit of profit the label stuck, and the lines were irrevocably drawn.

In many ways, business is quite happy to embrace the Philistine label, as it conforms to its self-image of seriousness and the hard-nosed domination of something it calls the 'real world'. At Penguin I encountered these divisions at first hand. My job was to preserve and promote the world's literary riches, yet within a commercial imprint ultimately answerable to Pearson's shareholders. And much more recently, I learnt that one of the reasons we had been unsuccessful in an Annual Report pitch I took part in was my reference to *Romeo and Juliet* during the pitch presentation. Shakespeare, it was felt, was not a fitting subject for the boardroom, or the serious business of investor relations. (To be fair, they also mentioned my suede shoes, the patches on my jacket sleeves, and the fact that I stood up and walked about a bit when I presented. Let's face it, they really didn't like me.) And so when I forsook the literary world for corporate branding, it was clear to me that I would need to leave all that soft stuff behind me. The two realms symbolised by my two CVs looked destined to remain separate forever.

But developments in my career and within the communications sphere have brought about their partial reconciliation. In 2008, I joined a communications agency based in Shoreditch, London called Radley Yeldar. They started out in Annual Reporting in 1986, and now work across a broad spectrum of communications, including Moving Image, Employee Engagement, Digital, Brand, and Sustainability communications. As the agency evolved it developed a common principle and philosophy to connect these skills. Story is that connection.

After all, they were pioneers in, what was back then, the new idea of 'narrative' reporting. This is where a company seeks to provide a coherent account of its performance through word and image, rather than just numbers. Standard practice now, but testimony to the fact that story plays a big part in Radley Yeldar's own story. And because it was also a big part of mine, I soon found myself working across all these disciplines and employing skills and knowledge I had relegated to my other CV. As story became the focus of my work again, I found a natural fit between what branding and communications sought to achieve, and what the greatest works of literature had in common. At Penguin I had seen how many of their big name authors – Tom Clancy, Nick Hornby, Maeve Binchy – made millions by the power of their names. I knew storytellers could be brands. I now realised brands could also be storytellers.

Clients were also starting to talk about 'story', and it was beginning to open doors that had been resolutely shut to 'brand'. I can't tell you how many times I've been pulled aside before entering a boardroom, and conspiratorially enjoined by a nervous marketing manager not to mention the 'B word' before the CEO. Brand, for all the claims and efforts of its professional advocates, is often still associated in the C-Suite with logos. The sole responsibility of the marketing department, to be interfered with and spent money on only under duress. Yet many of the very same companies where brand was a forbidden word were happy to talk openly about "getting their story straight". Happy to see it play a role very like that of brand in its more all-encompassing mission, but applied directly to a specific communications need.

Things are definitely changing, with 'story' becoming something of a buzzword in communications and marketing. In America it is even more established, with one recent book claiming that "many of the most successful organizations on the planet intentionally use storytelling as a key leadership tool". Yet there's still a long way to go over here. For if European companies are following their US counterparts by assigning a "high-level 'corporate storyteller' to capture and share their most important stories", then they are clearly keeping these stories to themselves. For every company that embraces storytelling there must be countless others who believe Shakespeare or similar has no place in the boardroom, or nothing to contribute to their world.

How story can help businesses communicate better is what this book is all about. Unlike many books designed for business audiences, mine does not claim to offer groundbreaking revelations or newly minted secrets to success. I have not seen the future, nor can I promise to get you there quicker. In fact, what I want to share is not new at all, rather, very old indeed. There are no secrets to impart. As Robert McKee puts it in his classic screenwriting primer *Story: Substance, Structure, Style and the Principles of Screenwriting* "In the twenty-three centuries since Aristotle wrote *The Poetics*, the 'secrets' of story have been as public as the library down the street".

Nor is there any mystery to why storytelling has a role in business communications. It belongs here because telling stories is part of what it means to be human. There is not a culture on this earth that does not tell, exchange and enjoy stories.

Story is simply effective communication. It allows humans to connect powerfully with each other, and share information about what it is to be human; whether they are sitting in the auditorium of a theatre, or behind the polished walnut table of a successful company. As a literary critic turned brand consultant/corporate storyteller, I do not seek to translate the secrets of one world into the other. Rather, I want to stress that there is only one world, and one basic psychology that has not evolved one jot since it became recognisably human, and started to share stories. Why they have this power, what they have in common, and what we can learn from this to help business communicate better, is what this book is about.

The following does not hail from my literary CV, nor from my communications one. But from a space where they connect and overlap. It is my belief that maintaining two CVs reflects false divisions and denies rich opportunities. I hope one day to make my two CVs one. That is the goal of the journey I now propose we take together.

# The Beginning

"Those who tell the stories rule society"
Plato, *The Republic*

# chapter one
# Why Story

---

Once upon a time, as *homo sapiens* started to group together in larger and more complex social units, they developed increasingly sophisticated ways to communicate. The more intelligent they became, the richer and more varied were the ideas they sought to share. First orally, with sounds and gestures, then with metaphors, figures of speech and mythical fables, as narrative started to take on a life of its own. Or pictorially, as preserved in the extraordinarily vivid cave paintings which speak to us eloquently about what was important to our preliterate ancestors. Hunting scenes painted on cave walls point to the primeval need for stories. Celebrating glories in the past, they imparted vital knowledge for the present, and ensured survival into the future.

Stories helped them become us.

# *Why we tell stories*

At its most basic, a story is an explanation. It helps us individually and collectively to make sense of the world. Some of the first stories explained why the sun rises; how it travels across the heavens each day (for the ancient Egyptians this was by boat, for the Greeks a fiery chariot); why the natural world dies each winter, and why it returns again in the spring. Cause and effect, however fanciful the explanation, is served by stories. Humans looked up, saw the stars sprinkling the heavens, and started to tell stories about them. They made connections between those distant luminous points, describing shapes that mirrored things from the world below, and spun yarns explaining how they got there, and their role and influence in their lives. The human brain loves to enquire, and loves to forge connections between things in its constant search for meaning. Narrative results from these needs.

Stories are literally as old as time itself. Time as a concept, linking past, present and future, beginning, middle and end, is simply the master narrative we've contrived to give our existence direction and meaning. Stories explain who we are, where we've come from, what's important to us, and where we are going. Jews, Christians and Muslims are collectively known as 'Children of the Book', because their sense of identity, their laws of conduct, and their destinies are enshrined in the stories that define their creeds. The Bible and the Koran show how stories can preserve collective memory down the centuries, and continue to influence cultures in a world far removed from that which brought these stories into being. Stories are the mainstays of identity and ideology.

For thousands of years the Bible provided the dominant narrative for explaining the world and its workings in the West. It was challenged, and largely replaced, by an alternative narrative in the nineteenth century. Evolutionary theory is currently the master story that unlocks the secrets of our being in fields as diverse as neurology and sociology, finance and politics. Although Darwin did his utmost to avoid implying there was an ultimate purpose in the workings of evolution, he was wasting his breath. A story needs a hero. And so Nature replaced God as the first and last principle. Happily evolved after.

Stories are powerful, potentially dangerous things. Dictators and despots love them, using myths of origin and destiny to justify their ideologies, and ruthlessly suppressing any stories that contradict their own. If they were merely decorative, frivolous fancies to entertain idle or immature brains, then the poets, authors and film-makers wouldn't be the first to be eliminated in political upheavals. Stories can mean the difference between life and death, justice and injustice. Picture a courtroom, a staple of dramatic fiction. A man's freedom, maybe his life, depends on his lawyer making a coherent case for his defence. There has to be a plausible thread between events, that hangs together logically, and answers important questions about motive and means. Judge and jury, who are instinctively disposed to look for narrative coherence, make momentous decisions based on which side told the most convincing story. Our survival, and day-to-day existence, depends on stories still.

Individual as much as collective identity is forged through this narrative impulse. We are constantly telling ourselves stories about ourselves. We are bound to our pasts by the thread of memory, and to our futures through anticipation, aspiration and daydream. So strong is the link between selfhood and narrative that practitioners in some schools of Cognitive Behaviour Therapy (CBT) focus on story as the basis of their therapeutic interventions. They help their patients break unhelpful behavioural patterns by encouraging them to recognise these self-defining narratives for what they are: merely stories. Therapists encourage patients to question the validity of these internal narratives as they would any other story they might hear – an item of news, a piece of gossip – from any external source. Story, for good or ill, defines who we are, and can determine the shape our lives take. We are all autobiographers, even if we never commit a word of our stories to paper.

We instinctively seek origin, order and direction in our lives, and use stories to forge relationships between things, events and one another. Our brains are wired to do this. Recent research in neuroscience suggests that we use stories as a way of filtering, digesting and making sense of information. So called 'Split-Brain' research affords insights on the brain's propensity for narrative. Studies have identified a function in the left hemisphere of the brain that's been labelled 'the interpreter'. Its role is to take the raw data supplied by the right half and make sense of it in narrative terms. Experiments found that patients with no neural link between left and right brain still had interpreters busily telling stories to make logical sense of fragments of information residing in the right brain. As Jonathan Gottschall puts it: "The left brain is a classic know-it-all; when it doesn't know the answer to a question, it can't bear to admit it. … it would rather fabricate a story than leave something unexplained".

Stories were our earliest form of instruction, both as a species and individuals. It was through stories that we first learned of a world beyond the narrow confines of our infantile existence. A world of imaginative possibilities, exotic beings, expansive landscapes, happy ever afters. They stretched our minds, excited our imaginations, encouraged receptiveness, and often instructed us in some moral or learning to take away, remember and apply later. They helped shape our ambitions, and prepared us for life. Deep, deep inside us remains a receptive bias to story as a form of instruction and inspiration. We open up to stories, when facts, figures and rational arguments fail to influence our heard-it-all-before adult brains. Story never sought to persuade us of anything overtly. Or, if it did, such as some moral instructing us in the ethical life, we probably didn't notice or care.

The tale had won us over. Some atavism from individual or collective memory is activated when we are told a story, an instinctive receptiveness responding to a deep human truth that still has the power to move us in any sphere of life.

The desire to share as much as to consume stories appears to be just as instinctive. It is fundamental to our existence as 'supersocial' animals. From, "it wasn't me, it was him", to "it's not you, it's me", we tell stories our whole lives through. Some of them are even true. From the headlines we consume with our breakfast, to the tales we read our children last thing at night, even beyond, to the dreams that pursue us while we sleep. There is not an hour of the day, a culture on the planet, or an area of experience untouched by story.

Including the world of business. Although it often needs reminding of this.

## Why business needs stories

Business, like any sphere of experience, has its own rules and rituals, its own language, and its own terms and conditions of engagement. And like the tribes we encountered earlier, with their fireside legends and cave paintings, it tells itself some pretty persuasive stories.

One of the most persistent is about how it operates in a world apart. A world ruled by a powerful deity called Reason, who bestowed on it a magic talisman called Analytics to guide it through a challenging, sometimes treacherous, territory called the Markets to a promised land of undreamed of wealth called Value. Business has slain its fair share of dragons in the past, and is aware that its distinct identity was forged by triumphing over those who would threaten this destiny. There were those foes I mentioned earlier when I explained how the divisions between culture and commerce became entrenched in the industrial revolution. Whilst the aristocracy looked to the past to define itself, through the preservation of inherited wealth and tradition, the commercial classes embraced the future, putting their faith in what could be made, measured and marketed. Laws were repealed, restrictions on trade lifted, and slowly but surely the markets held sway. Interestingly, the Utilitarian philosophy which spurred these socio-economic upheavals labelled the beliefs of those who would defend their ancient privileges 'fictions'. 'Fictions' were irrational, appealing to sentiment, tradition and custom, to be replaced by a rational calculus of collective value. The bottom line became the ultimate Holy Grail, and Adam Smith is venerated still by free market economists as a founding father of their tribe.

Business, trade, commerce defined itself through such victories, assured of what it was in conscious opposition to what it was not. Business still largely sees itself as a world set apart, where there is no room for 'fictions', and the soft, woolly sentiments a word like 'story' might imply. Here are some of the objections business might raise to keep story out of its dominions:

*Business is ruled by reason, figures on spreadsheets not figures of speech. Story appeals to emotional, perhaps even irrational, impulses.*

*Business audiences are impatient, time-poor, cynical and only interested in facts and figures. Stories are for entertainment, enjoyment and therefore leisure time outside of office hours.*

*Business deals with and even defines (economic) reality, it must be trustworthy, open and authentic. Stories are fabulous, and deal with ideals rather than realities, lies rather than truths.*

Such objections might appear plausible if repeated enough. Yet they are only half-truths. Fictions in their own right, serving the massive collective denial sustaining the notion of a separate business world. Whilst it is perfectly acceptable for a fictional series like *Star Trek* to fantasise about a Vulcan planet governed exclusively by reason, there is no place for such fables in the real world of human beings, who use their whole brains when they think, choose and act, and who have been consuming and sharing stories their entire lives.

Business people are not Vulcans, whilst the financial markets which constitute their special realm of influence, are some of the most irrational and emotionally volatile regions of this earthling planet. Sentiment reigns supreme here, to be harnessed, steered and directed under a smokescreen of analytics. Stories do indeed appeal pre-eminently to emotions, which is why they should be deployed more effectively in the service of business communications, where a hell of a lot is riding on them. For it is emotion rather than reason that moves people. Moves them in the literal sense of compelling them to act – the ultimate purpose of any commercial communication. And it is on the emotional level that trust is built. A commodity, currently in desperately short supply.

Stories often work on the unconscious level, influencing areas immune or resistant to the facts and figures in which business puts such superstitious store. Take the idea of 'integrity'. This is a popular theme in the business world, with nearly every company (including Enron) listing it among its values. There are more effective and convincing ways to demonstrate integrity than simply talking about it. One of these is telling a coherent story. Integrity literally means 'holding together'. A building has structural integrity if all its parts hold together and support each other. A person has integrity if he or she demonstrates moral wholeness, with what they say and do matching up. Stories need integrity too. The thread holding all the parts together in a logical satisfying order, without which they just don't add up. How many times have you left a cinema not entirely satisfied with the film's ending? A broken thread, a vital scene missing that might have explained all. But the film lacked narrative integrity.

There's a reason why integrity is such a vital concept; but it needs to be demonstrated not discussed. Remember the courtroom drama, where life and freedom depend on a coherent story being made about a man's conduct and integrity. A similar case can be made for a business, demonstrating integrity far more effectively through a coherent story than simply listing the word among its values. Story helps to reveal who you really are through what you say and how you say it.

Business audiences are indeed time poor and impatient. Which is why effective storytelling perfectly serves their needs. Story provides the clarity, concision and focus to hook an audience's attention, and a thread to hold it there long enough to get your point across. Remember the cerebral 'interpreter' working away in the brain's left hemisphere, trying to make sense of data by turning facts into coherent narrative. Save it time, help it out. A child doesn't say "read me a list daddy", nor do our sham Vulcans in pinstripes, whatever they may believe or claim. It is precisely because these audiences have not elected to be told a story, and have little time and patience to waste, that you need to use the sharpest tools at your disposal to cut through these barriers. Story, sharpened to perfection through millennia, provides these tools.

Finally, story's association with the world of entertainment should hardly encourage us to segregate creativity and commerce. Their successful partnership in an institution like Hollywood should be reason enough for business to take storytelling very seriously, and be prepared to learn from the commercial masters of the craft. Hollywood is, after all, a highly effective machine for turning stories into dollars. It has made vast riches from making narrative an almost exact science, establishing principles for screenwriting that are applied in movie after movie. Story by numbers, perhaps, but it makes the numbers.

The public that seeks story for entertainment is made up of individuals who also buy products and services, put on suits and go to work, seek information, exchange information, analyse companies, speculate on their possible futures, buy and sell companies and justify these actions in narrative accounts, they gossip, joke, banter, surf the internet, read the paper, read stories to their children, watch TV, read a few pages of a book, dream. Entertainment stories simply exploit for commercial ends this voracious, ubiquitous need for narrative. Something we do instinctively when we forget we are 'at work', or 'doing business'. Story is whole-brain thinking. Its desire for clarity demands intellectual and analytical rigour; its desire for narrative coherence seeks logical order; and its emotional resonance moves people. By moving people you make them act. The captains of commerce neglect a very powerful tool if they believe story is simply about irrational entertainment, and has no role to play in their world. Ultimately there is no separate world. That is just a story.

By rejecting these distinctions, and denying these denials, story can help business communicate much more effectively. The world of business cannot pretend to be immune to the power of storytelling. But by understanding its principles, and applying them consistently, it can simply do this a whole lot better. Business, a world set apart, a planet protected by force fields of denial, may be the final frontier for story.

We can now boldly go into that world. Armed with the arts of effective storytelling.

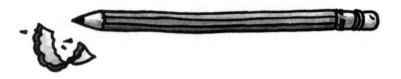

## *Why brands tell stories*

But before we go much further, I should explain what I mean by corporate storytelling.

Unlike its corporate counterpart, Business-to-Consumer marketing rarely forgets it is talking to living, breathing, feeling, irrational and occasionally rational beings. Consequently it has far more readily embraced storytelling. Consumer advertising is unashamedly about telling stories. This is especially so in the UK, where the British literary heritage and discomfort with US style hard sell have turned the vulgar business of selling stuff into a narrative art form. So much so that the lines between entertainment and promotion often become blurred. As they were in the classic Nescafé Gold TV commercials of the 1980s and 90s, where a romantic saga of two nauseating yuppies with no taste in coffee was followed as avidly as a soap opera in its own right. The long-running Hovis ads have been serving up short slices of cosy nostalgia for generations. Whilst Compare the Meerkat taps into the British love of surreal silliness to enliven a dull product with catchphrase comedy sketches. At the other extreme there is the epic grandeur of the award-winning 'White Horses' Guinness commercial, featuring lines from *Moby Dick*, through to the knowing wordplay of the *Economist* print ads. British advertising tends to gravitate towards the literary, showing that this nation of shopkeepers is also a nation of storytellers. It is no accident that some of the biggest names in British film-making cut their directorial teeth in advertising. David Puttnam, Alan Parker and Ridley Scott told their first cinematic stories on much smaller screens.

Consumer brands know how to build relationships by telling stories. Not just about products, but sometimes about the companies behind them. Some are so successful at this that their stories have become legends, and there is even a whole series of books showcasing such famous brand stories. Guinness, Google and Innocent are all given this treatment, as well as Premium Bonds, Brand America and even David Beckham.

Innocent is a textbook example of building brand devotion through language, humour and storytelling, as recounted in John Simmons' excellent book about the company and the brand in the Great Brand Stories series. Everything about the Innocent brand flows from the legend of its inception. Three friends working far too hard in London wanted to find healthy alternatives to the usual lunchtime fodder. They decided what the world needed was pure fruit smoothies. In 1998 they made a batch to sell at London's Notting Hill Carnival. Whilst the heroes of ancient legends consulted the Delphic Oracle to determine their destinies, their modern equivalents did a bit of market testing. They simply asked their customers to vote whether these three Innocents of business should give up their day jobs and dedicate themselves to their smoothie dreams. The answer was, of course, a resounding yes, and the rest is very successful business history, and a wonderfully consistent brand story too. Innocent by name, packaging, tone of voice and personality.

Innocent is legendary for its quirky humour, which many have attempted to imitate with diminishing degrees of success. Silly quips on the packaging, such as my favourite: "Separation may occur (but mummy still loves daddy)", endear us to the products and their producers, and make us want to be part of their story. We feel it is authentically 'them', the people behind the products, with a true story and a genuine voice that makes a genuine emotional connection. Their approach to nutrition (using only pure ingredients or explaining why this is difficult), aligns with their various social equity initiatives, and, back in the day, Fruitstock, the free festival they staged in Regent's Park, upon which the sun shone every year, I fondly recall. The company carries this attitude through consistently even to City relations, refusing to adopt a different personality just because it's talking to the 'grown ups' on planet business. They may be 'hippies with calculators' as some have claimed, but they don't talk like calculators. This, for me, is as refreshing as their products. It's what a clear and consistent story allows a company like Innocent to do, blurring the lines between B2C and B2B communications, and so demonstrating that such distinctions are not really all that helpful. A storytelling mindset helps break them down.

Not every brand story has to be based on a founding legend. Such legends can be truly inspiring if you are a brand devotee, or just plain depressing if you are a competitor lacking a similarly compelling tale. Attempt to follow suit without the substance (as Innocent's imitators have done with off-the-shelf quirkiness), and there's the risk that your own lack-lustre legend is about as interesting as someone else's dream or holiday snaps. Unless where you have come from defines what you are about now, and where you are going in the future, and there is still a direct benefit in this for your stakeholders, then it's best that you keep the story of your inception to yourself.

This legendary emphasis slightly distorts the role of storytelling in corporate communications. We are often told that every great brand has a great story behind it. This may be true; but there are a few with uninspiring beginnings, and some with origins best not mentioned at all (Volkswagen's links to Nazi Germany to name only the most obvious). I'm less concerned with the stories *behind* great brands, so much as those put to the fore – behind which the business must itself stand. Story as an articulation of what the brand is all about, not just where it has come from; what it has to offer, and why this is relevant to its core audiences in the world today.

In fact, some of the most successful brands and brand stories say very little about the companies themselves, and everything about their audiences. They are not about what the company has done and where it came from, but about what their customers could do, and where the brand might take them. Nike's 'Just Do It' is a supreme example of such storytelling at work. What 'it' may be depends on the aspirations of each individual, whose personal stories become part of the company's own.

These principles hold true for business to business brands as much as their more seductive B2C counterparts. Even more so. Without a product that directly touches the everyday lives of consumers, you have to work harder to get your message across. Story helps this happen, as an example from my own experience at Radley Yeldar I hope demonstrates.

In 2009, a European IT and Business Services company called Steria celebrated its 40th anniversary. They asked us to help them commemorate this with a publication. Originally the idea was for a coffee table book narrating their corporate history. Founded in Paris in 1969, Steria emerged out of that maelstrom of radical unrest with a mission to use the nascent science of information technology as a force for social good. But that was then, and the world has moved on. It was essential that this celebratory publication told a story that was relevant to its audiences today, or it simply looks self-congratulatory. Whilst 40 is pretty impressive (especially in the world of IT), and worth commemorating, the figure itself is somewhat arbitrary, and a mere stripling compared to the 100, 125 and 140 years celebrated by Selfridges, Marks & Spencer and Sainsbury's that very same year.

We proposed that '1' was a far more significant number in Steria's story than 40, pointing to the many firsts to which the company could lay claim. The book would feature a selection of these from throughout the decades, positioning Steria as a serial pioneer, but talking about the world it had helped to change and was still changing, rather than all about the company itself. There was the first pocket calculator; something resembling a word-processing solution many years before Microsoft; even a prototype of the Internet. Gems that might have remained buried in the dense pages of a linear corporate history book were unearthed, polished and showcased as individual stories. Combined they told an impressive tale of innovation, brought to life by examples everyone can recognise as part of the fabric of our lives today.

Steria is a classic B2B company, quietly doing complex, sometimes obscure and technical, things behind the scenes of everyday life. Yet it had a powerful story to share, communicating a clear and a relevant benefit to the companies it helps, and the lives of the public those companies in turn serve. The likes of Steria often have to work harder to tell their stories than their B2C equivalents. But when they do, the prize is clearer, more compelling communications.

## *Why brand needs story*

Story crosses borders, reconciling supposed opposites, and eroding false distinctions. What works in entertainment works just as well in a world that has set itself deliberately apart. What works for Business-to-Consumer brands and communications, applies equally to their corporate counterparts. B2C? B2B? Story transcends such distinctions, belonging to the universal regions of Human-to-Human connections.

Brand and story were made for each other. They have an awful lot in common. Yet story has a number of advantages over this relative latecomer, and can more effectively fulfil many of the promises made in brand's name. The corporate brand is something of a paradox. On the one hand it is everywhere, summing up and expressing everything people should think and feel about an organisation. It is something to be experienced at every point of contact, and 'lived' by every member of the organisation that owns it. This is brand as concept, somehow more than the sum of its parts, and residing intangibly in the realm of ideas and emotions. And yet, because it is also something that is owned, it also needs to be controlled, regulated, codified and policed. Brand bibles and guidelines are developed, to be enforced by brand police. Messages, images, behaviours can be on or off brand. And so, despite claims for its ubiquity, brand still has to belong somewhere, usually the marketing department, whose professional expertise makes the folk there responsible for making the conceptual real. Their responsibility, their budget, their problem.

Story, on the other hand, really does belong everywhere and can be participated in by everyone. I could describe a brand to you, detail it in a brand book or guidelines, specify its colours and symbols, explain the behaviour expected of it in adjectives, but you would still only have these abstract signifiers. Not the thing itself. If I tell you a story, you have it. It's yours as well as mine; it comes alive in your imagination. Whilst most books about branding feel compelled to offer their own (roughly similar) definition of the concept, there is no real need to do the same with story. Everyone knows what we mean by story, for everyone participates in its exchange – what Robert McKee calls "the currency of human contact". Story carries the rational and emotional freight brand deals in, and so makes the conceptual real and relevant. It can do this because of the human impulse to exchange and connect through narrative.

Ok. Think of a brand. The first one that comes into your head. Why that one? If you think about it, it's likely that this brand has had an impact on you (for good or ill). And it's also likely that you have some anecdote associated with this impact already formed, or steadily forming, in your mind. It might be nostalgic recall, or some sudden epiphany that now defines forever your impression of that brand and the associations it carries. These associations in turn inform expectations of it in the future. That is how brands work. If you share this anecdote, it becomes a story that explains why you feel the way you do about this brand. A story that has far greater currency than anything its official promoters are able to say about it. Word of mouth, long recognised as the most effective form of advertising, is all about sharing stories, with social media making advocacy the most powerful brand communicator imaginable.

Brand ends up living and communicating through story. It is the currency of its meaning; so thinking about it in narrative terms from the offset gives it a greater chance of achieving the anecdotal advocacy that truly gives it life. If brands seek to live in the hearts and minds of individuals, story provides the royal road to those regions, travelling along synaptic pathways worn smooth by eons of communication practice. As Mike Oliver, Head of Brand at Radley Yeldar puts it: "Brands help people understand you, remember you and do business with you". Story just makes this easier to happen. Story is about having something to say, not just something to sell. A point of view as well as a point of difference.

## *Why now?*

Storytelling is as old as history. Branding as a concept and commercial practice is relatively new, as a professional discipline newer still. Why has it taken so long to recognise and exploit what I'm claiming is obvious, universal and instinctive? Why is storytelling now firmly on the corporate agenda, with clients asking for it, agencies supplying it, and publishers publishing books about it? To answer this, it's worth reminding ourselves of the history of branding, and where this converges with the much older history of story.

Story, as I've argued, fulfils a fundamental human need. Brands emerged much later in response to problems brought about by historical circumstances. Whilst there had been forerunners of brands in the political and religious spheres, with their symbols, shields and slogans, brands as we know and use them today emerged, like so many things I've been discussing, in the industrial epoch. Industry vastly accelerated the production, proliferation and circulation of goods. This created greater choice, more competition, and thus brought about the need for brands to help people make choices between these competing products.

Trust is the need brands evolved to serve in this new epoch of industry and urbanisation. People who lived in villages or urban neighbourhoods traditionally knew who and what to trust. They knew the baker, the brewer and the chandler, and they knew the quality of their bread, beer, candles or soap. Personal knowledge born of experience helped to regulate commerce. Urbanisation uprooted populations and threw them into new unknown environments in unprecedented numbers very quickly. When people came to buy products they didn't know who or what to trust. Brands stepped in to help, as guarantors of provenance and consistency of product. People then developed relationships with these surrogates for personal knowledge. Symbols were devised to make recognition and ownership easier. Experience of a product bearing that symbol encouraged expectation of the same quality being fulfilled in the present and the future. Branding codifies cause and effect, anticipation and realisation in each transaction. It slips naturally into narrative. The brain forms stories around brands, as it does around all experiences.

Trust is a fundamental need of any social unit, the glue of any tribe. Trust is also a major role and outcome of storytelling for our species. Stories have a tacit policing function, regulating societies through the exchange and circulation of gossip. In a pre-urban society you not only knew about the quality of the baker's product, you probably knew a lot about his conduct too. You might hear a rumour that he was adulterating his flour (or even the chandler's wife), and decide to take your custom elsewhere (or not, if you were the frustrated brewer's wife and wanting a slice of the baker's action). Stories, in the form of gossip, were the informal communications currency regulating society, and also commerce before brands came into being.

As an interesting aside, the epoch that gave birth to brands as symbolic surrogates for personal knowledge, also saw the rise of detective fiction, a genre shaped by similar needs and circumstances. Detective fiction, as perfected by Wilkie Collins, Robert Louis Stevenson and Arthur Conan Doyle's Sherlock Holmes stories, emerged, like branding, out of the new urban industrial context, and the needs and anxieties it created. If brands came into being because city-dwelling consumers didn't know *what* to trust, detective stories became popular because in cities no one knew *whom* to trust. In a city everyone was a stranger. New identities could be assumed, criminal pasts obscured, requiring the new figure of the detective to fathom the city and its mysteries.

Organised police forces, criminology, criminal records, detectives and detective fiction were all entirely new phenomena, emerging in the last decades of the nineteenth century. So many of the Sherlock Holmes stories deal with assumed and obscured identities. 'The Man with the Twisted Lip' is a classic example, all about a City banker who finds begging more lucrative than banking, and so amasses a fortune from deception (imagine that!). Individual identity is the problematic of detective fiction; as corporate identity is that of business communications. In 1886 the UK's first trademark was registered. In the following year the first Sherlock Holmes story was published. Both events mark milestones in what might be called the cultural history of trust. Both the detective story and the branding story emerge from the problems of identity: whom or what to trust. (But I digress. What can you expect from a literary historian turned brand consultant?)

If the technological innovations that changed the face of modern society in the industrial epoch gave birth to brands, so the information technology that is changing our worlds anew might explain why we are embracing storytelling to help us navigate new unknowns.

Industrialisation and urbanisation quite literally changed the landscape of society, creating an urgent need for new symbols and narratives to restore trust in alien, anonymous environments. Trust is as critical today as it's ever been, in a similarly disorientating world. The landscape we now need to negotiate has expanded to include the constantly changing and potentially infinite regions of hyperspace. Everything about how we communicate, including how we communicate about brands, is up for grabs. It is not surprising that we might feel the need to reach for established practices. Story is thus newly relevant, providing a familiar thread to guide us through the labyrinth of new unknowns.

The more the rules appear to be re-written, the more we rely on the old ones, operating just beneath the surface to keep us steadily on our course. 'User Experience' (UX) is an established function of digital communications, a vital component for any robust web development strategy. Its domain is 'navigation', an old term, serving an old need within a radically new environment. The first navigators used the stars to help them keep course, and told stories about them. And despite the non-linear narratives the web gives rise to, there is still a need for clear and coherent threads for our journeys. 'Breadcrumbs' is another charming term used in digital communications, providing the same role in web design as it did to help Hansel and Gretel in the folk tale. We all still need ways through the woods, threads through the labyrinths. Story still provides those threads, tying us to the past through unchanging human needs.

The complexity of modern communications obscures but doesn't eradicate fundamental human needs, or the tried and tested means of fulfilling them. Trust, belief, belonging, identity, affirmation, progression, goals, problem-solving: all these things our brains instinctively seek, and devise ways of finding them and communicating them. The world changes, but the ways to navigate it do not fundamentally change. If brands emerged to supply the means to trust in a new commercial reality, then the erosion of that trust in the modern corporate environment creates a new challenge for brands, and a new need for story to help form the human connections upon which trust is built.

This is why story, as old as time itself, has a new and vital currency. Story has currency because currency, exchange, and the open circulation and exchange of ideas and stories is a condition of our evermore connected world. A connected world encourages and demands a currency of connection. Story, perhaps *the* universal human principle, provides that currency.

Story as a means of communication can bring us all closer. The global village is largely a fiction, a mirage of wishful economic thinking. Or it could be a reality brought about through communications fulfilling the universal desire to share stories. Inhabiting that village allows us all to trade gossip, anecdote, and instant intelligence on vastly unprecedented scales. The campfire or marketplace around which we congregate may be bigger and more dispersed, but the needs it fulfils, and the means to fulfil them, have not changed one jot. This is the premise and purpose of this book: using the old to help us make sense of the ever new.

# *Why another book on the subject?*

This is not the first book to suggest companies might usefully adopt the art of storytelling. (Indeed, in the time it took to write this book it became a veritable torrent.) In the United States storytelling is a well-established leadership tool, with books such as Stephen Denning's '*The Leader's Guide to Storytelling*' (2005) encouraging executives to exchange tables for fables when seeking to persuade. For every challenge there is the right story, and Denning, and more recently Paul Smith's *Lead With A Story* (2012), provide persuasive arguments and good-to-go examples and templates to bring story into the regions where analytics have traditionally reigned. For these writers story is a 'Leadership Discipline', to be deployed whenever and wherever it is needed.

For me story is an ethos to be embraced before it is a template to apply. Adherence to the latter runs the risk of obscuring the naturalness of story as something in which we all instinctively participate. Story doesn't carry a TM symbol, and there are no hidden secrets to its power. The only secret is to remember this when we put that novel and newspaper into our bags, and switch on our computers at work. I do not address my book only to 'Leaders', but to human beings, regardless of the titles they are given or the professional statuses they assume.

My own approach is close to John Simmons' in this respect, whose crusade for making business communications more human is inspirationally pursued in such books as *We, Me, Them and It*, and *The Invisible Grail*. Through his books and workshops Simmons encourages individuals to bring their personalities to work in their business writing, thus making businesses more human and their brands more individual. I was on the receiving end of one of his workshops many years ago, and remember the thrill of seeing people who had no idea they could write find their voices by remembering personal stories, and sharing them with the group. As Simmons explains: "Poetry and storytelling [makes] the connection between two worlds – the individual and the corporate".

Making these connections is what story does best; creating what Simmons calls a 'bridge' between our personal and professional selves. Story is perhaps the only cultural practice every human on the planet has in common. If it is a bridge, it is a uniquely powerful and enduring one, spanning across time and diverse cultures. Understanding the principles of this power, and putting them to work – at work – is what my own book is all about.

This book seeks to provide an introduction to the principles of storytelling as applied to the corporate context. This is principally to serve a brand-building function, because of the natural fit between the objectives of one and the characteristics of the other. By remembering we are all instinctive and inveterate storytellers, we can simplify the daunting and usually over-complicated task of talking about business. By forgetting that there are separate worlds of 'leadership' and 'storytelling', and by remembering a few principles used by those who excel in this art, storytelling can become second nature for those who seek to simply communicate better for and about business.

Whilst I'm keen to stress the obviousness of story as applied to any communication task, there would be no need for this book if there were not a few principles to be laid down and adopted. It is perhaps because story is so obvious that it is in danger of being taken for granted or confined to the literary shelf. It is to that shelf I reach for guidance. Not because fiction and cinema exclusively own storytelling; but because these fields exemplify the craft as a conscious and highly effective practice. We can learn a lot about communicating and about ourselves by studying and borrowing the principles that make the greatest stories so powerful and enduring.

I should explain here, this is not a book just about writing, a how-to primer on producing sparkling copy. There are plenty of those about, and some of them quite excellent. It's about thinking as much as creating; acting as well as talking story. Story is not a literary, but a living art, which is why it is needed in a world that claims to be the 'real' one. The art of story reflects and makes real that world. It gives shape to something that doesn't actually have a shape: 'life'. It helps it make sense. The stories that should flow from rethinking the task of corporate communications will certainly benefit from understanding this art, and be better crafted as a consequence. Yet it is the understanding of what story is about, and the application of this to the process as much as the products of corporate communications, that I promote in these pages. We cannot all be professional writers, but we are all already storytellers. We can all do this a little better by studying the age-old art of storytelling.

This book explains how. The first part seeks to explain how story, as a mindset and a set of universal principles, can assist the business of corporate brand building. The middle shows how storytelling as a discipline can help bring that brand to life through clear, coherent and compelling communications. And then a short denouement looks at where corporate storytelling appears to be going in the already emerging future.

# The landscape of storytelling

I've resisted the usual business book imperative to create elaborate models for concepts, but it's quite useful to map out the territory I will be exploring as a diagram.

At one extreme is a sphere I have called the *Story Impulse*. This represents the everyday world of storytelling most of humanity indulges in naturally, even unconsciously, every single day. This is storytelling in its most basic, unstructured form, with roots that go very deep into the origins of human kind. Whilst it is low on structure, being an informal, instinctive practice most of us do, it is high on credibility, and acceptability. The stories exchanged in this sphere we generally accept to be true, and readily welcome into our lives. Gossip is the most representative form of this type of storytelling.

The second sphere, which I've entitled the *Story Business*, is far more structured, formal and professional than the first. It employs story as a conscious practice, benefiting from rules and principles which exploit for pleasure and profit the same impulses that reside in the first sphere. Whilst these types of stories are more consciously structured, we are less inclined to believe in them as literal truths, precisely because they employ formal aesthetic conventions we are prepared to accept as part of the deal. Samuel Taylor Coleridge called this acceptance "the willing suspension of disbelief" audiences were prepared to concede to fiction for the pleasure it gives us. While we know they're not true, we still welcome and actively seek these stories out. Any form of fiction, be it literary, cinematic, or dramatic, characterises storytelling in this sphere.

The third sphere I've called the *Business Story*. This contains all the arts of communication in the service of commerce. Like the second sphere it is characterised by a high degree of professionalism, but varying degrees of structure and formalism. The rules of this sphere are less associated with aesthetics – the principles of good storytelling belonging to the second sphere – so much as ethics – deriving from a rigidly defined and severely restricted sense of professional propriety. Where the *Business Story* borders with the *Story Business* we find the more imaginative arts of B2C narrative practice, which willingly embraces many of its neighbour's customs. At the further extreme, in splendid isolation, resides the corporate 'story'. By removing itself as far as possible from the world of the first sphere, corporate communications reinforces the sense that it lives in, and talks to, a world set apart. Jargon is its characteristic form, signalling its isolation.

This 'professional' isolation paradoxically removes it from both the structured world of the *Story Business* (because that deals with fictions and untruths), as well as the unstructured world of the everyday informal exchange of stories. The more professional it attempts to be, the more barriers it constructs to keep these worlds at bay, the more distance it puts between itself and those other spheres. Despite its high professionalism it is only semi-structured or conscious in its storytelling and quite low on credibility and acceptance. It prefers logic over emotion; lists over narrative. And so, too often, it is not really storytelling at all. And whilst this sphere has voluntarily isolated itself from the world of the first sphere, the audiences it needs to reach are made up of people from that world. These people informally enjoy and share stories, and willingly seek out those issuing from the *Story Business*. That is to say, human beings. These are the people it ultimately depends on, to sell its stuff and its stories to.

The remedy I propose is found in this book. I will argue that the best way for the third sphere to connect with the first is to adopt some of the structures of the second. By embracing the principles of storytelling perfected in this realm, it might just start to establish a closer connection with the world it ultimately needs to reach. The *Business Story* needs to embrace the *Story Business* if it is to achieve its objectives. How it might usefully achieve this is in the following pages.

# chapter two
# What Makes a Story

———

As I suggested earlier, there is no real secret to what makes a story 'a Story' and most experts on the narrative craft tend to agree on its essential ingredients. For the purposes of using story as a brand and communications discipline, I've boiled these essential ingredients down to three: clarity, coherence and emotional connection. My aim is to make storytelling in this context as intuitive to practice as it is to identify in the works that move us in any medium. For me the essentials of good practice are found in clarity of theme, coherence of thread and the ability to connect emotionally. Bring these things to your communications practice and you are starting to tell a story.

# *Clarity*

When I was the editor of the Penguin Classics series I was constantly being asked to define what makes a work a Classic. The series is very diverse, comprising well over a thousand works of fiction, poetry, philosophy, religion and history from all ages and cultures. Yet they were all labelled 'Classics', meaning they had something in common. The answer is still relevant to the job I do today. For what defines a Classic is what makes a compelling story in any field.

A Classic in any medium is a work that endures. It survives the test of time and translates from one language and culture into another. The greatest works from Homer to Hardy, *Gilgamesh* to *The Great Gatsby*, allow readers to recognise through the external circumstances of period and place a common humanity. These works still speak to people, through time and across space, offering relevant universal truths. That is why they remain Classics, sell in large volumes, and are kept in print by Penguin.

At the core of a Classic, and at the core of a compelling story, is an easily identifiable theme. Archetypes tend to be classified at the thematic level, and can be defined in a sentence. Classics continue to appeal because a central human drama is clearly identifiable under all that fancy dress and foreign circumstance. Boy meets girl. Girl's parents disapprove, or class, nationality and circumstance get in their way. If they eventually overcome these obstacles (and it's starring Sarah Jessica Parker) then you have a romantic comedy. If they fail you have tragedy. (This, incidentally, explains my own ill-fated *Romeo and Juliet* reference in that boardroom. I was simply, as now, trying to explain the need for clarity and focus in how a complex business presents its story.)

Clarity is therefore the first essential of storytelling. For a Classic work, it's what gives it universal appeal and staying power. For new works, those potential future Classics, it's what gives them an earthly chance of being noticed, published and promoted. Publishing is an essentially conservative industry, averse to taking risks. When books are bought by publishing houses (and they are bought by the publishers long before they reach the book shop shelves), they tend to fall into recognisable genres. This makes it easier for the publishers to promote the works, the bookshops to shelve them, or Amazon to classify them, and the public to want them. It's even been claimed that there are only *Seven Basic Plots* (the title of Christopher Brooker's exhaustively encyclopaedic classification of the canon proving this). Publishing is conservative, because the book-buying public is. The book-buying public is because the human mind is, seeking recognisable patterns with enough intriguing variation to reward its attention.

Cinema deals so consistently in archetypes, it makes the claim that there might be as many as even seven plots seems positively profligate. It has turned the business of storytelling into almost an exact science, as well as a highly lucrative commercial enterprise. It is therefore to the movies that I generally turn when seeking to persuade business of the commercial advantages of effective storytelling. And if business audiences are as time-poor, cynical, and attention deficient as we have grounds to suspect, they find their counterpart, if not their match, in the hard-nosed, thick-skinned money men from movie land.

Remember the very funny Orange cinema ads from a few years back? A series of Hollywood stars, ranging from John Cleese to Darth Vader, try to pitch story ideas to a smart-arsed, wisecracking Orange exec, who has his own agenda. He is only interested in promoting Orange products, and so has no time for the poor schlub trying to get his or her story idea across. Imagine you are talking to this guy when you are trying to get people interested in your own story. Now, I'm not suggesting for a moment that the nice people you want to do business with are really like this chief idiot and his band of toadies. But his impatience, his preoccupations and his gnat-like attention span, can help us develop the discipline of clarity, concision and focus essential to storytelling. The hapless victims in the ads have about a nanosecond to get their story across in a single sentence. Could you do the same? If your business were a movie, what would the poster or trailer declare to have them queuing round the block? (a question I return to in earnest later). Corporate communications have a similar task as those movie posters and trailers: to promote their 'product' (their company), and a similar need for cynicism-busting, attention-grabbing clarity. This is the first fundamental for any story in any context.

Story's need for clarity and focus is one of the main things it shares with brand, and one of the reasons storytelling and brand building were made for each other. The most successful brands as much as the most powerful and enduring stories have this clarity. If you can sum your offer up in a short, snappy sentence, better still a word, then you also have the makings of a strong brand. Product brands have a clear advantage in this respect. They are often created to deliver a defined need, or fill a perceived gap. As that gap is likely to be wafer thin, their focus has to be razor sharp. Corporate brands are generally a lot more complex. They carry a lot more heritage, are answerable to many more people, and so often show reluctance in pinning themselves to a single idea. It's complicated, they object, and we have so many different audiences to satisfy and communicate with.

Which is precisely why they have to work a whole lot harder to get their offer across, and precisely why story is so useful here. Simplification is one of the hardest things to achieve in any sphere, but generally the most needed. Storytelling is partly an exercise in simplification. As Robert McKee puts it, "stories are metaphors for life". They take the messy, complicated, often contradictory stuff in which we are all immersed, and give it meaningful shape. Through selection of focus – an individual life or relationship serving as a metaphor for all life – understanding is gained. And life, albeit briefly, makes perfect sense.

Stories are made for this. They are great for imparting knowledge and influencing behaviour. Socrates, Christ and The Buddha all used parables for this purpose, instructing disciples in a moral precept or ideal course of action far more effectively through story than by serving up dogma directly. Because a parable has a core lesson it has to have a single focus, clearly using the ostensible subject – a shepherd, a man living in a cave – to be translatable to the listener's own frame of reference.

Stories are perfect for teaching, preaching and propaganda because they harness the clarity of a well-told tale to deliver an unambiguous message to effect a singularly defined outcome. Obama had excellent speechwriters, he had charisma, he knew how to mobilise social media, and America (the world), urgently needed change. But he also had a single-minded story to tell, iconically expressed in one emotive word HOPE. His speeches, his persona, his "Yes we can" rallying cry summed up this one single idea. Both promise and call to action. Hope. If a superpower's future can be defined so succinctly, a company can surely follow suit. You may do an awful lot, it may be awfully complicated, and you may have a lot of audiences. But you can't say everything to everyone all the time, nor should you try. What you do might not actually be the most compelling thing about you, or the best focus for your story. It often isn't.

This was brought home to me quite recently when a technology company asked us to redesign their website. They worked at the interface between banking and mobile technology, so their website had to command authority and credibility in its functionality. But it also had to be clear in its story if it was to convince its customers – mostly banks – of the superiority of the company's product against a handful of competitors. They had something different, potentially five years ahead of the game, and they were very proud of it. They just had difficulty getting those they needed to convince to grasp what made it so different. As the MD confessed, exasperatingly, at an early meeting, he had spent two years of funding rounds trying to explain what their kit of stuff does. That, I suggested, was where the problem lay. Stop trying to explain what it does, I suggested. Explain *why* this matters, and use this as the focus of your story.

So I devised an intensive whole day messaging 'Boot Camp', and refused to allow the core client team out of the building until I, the technical idiot, could understand and explain why anyone should care about their 'mobile payment ecosystem'. Which meant explaining what it would mean for their customers and their customers' customers in turn. This would be the core of their story and the top line message for their homepage, summing up their offer in terms of tangible benefits anyone could grasp or get excited about.

I wouldn't pretend this was easy. What with technology and finance there were many strata of jargon to drill through before we got down to the human core of their offer. But I kept on drilling, and the more I probed, the more exciting it became. For my constant challenging refrain of "so what?" forced them to describe what the future might be like if the major banks used their technology. A technology which uniquely enabled any mobile phone, anywhere in the world to process payments instantly instead of using cash or credit cards. As there are more mobile telephones in the world than toothbrushes (an interesting fact I learned that day), and vastly more than there are bank accounts or bank branches, this meant that the world's 'unbanked' populations could buy and sell, and be paid their wages. This was potentially attractive for their banking clients, and quite revolutionary for the rest of the world.

We started to image a cashless, credit-card-less world, where the humble mobile would do away with even the need for wallets. If film trailers can grab our attentions and fire our imaginations by asking us to "Imagine a world where…" why not a website promoting a revolutionary piece of technology that could bring about cashless commerce in just a few years? From barter, to coins to notes, to cheques to cards, there had been relatively few major changes in the history of money. Our client had what would deliver the next payment paradigm. That's pretty epic stuff, and demands a similarly confident story.

The Future of Money is Mobile. The Future of Mobile was in our client's hands. Five years ahead of the competition and ready to transform the way the world pays. And that is the story we went with.

It provided a key to unlock all the complexity of what they did, which only they, and the technical people at the banks, needed to fully understand. But these weren't the people they needed to reach first and foremost. It was rather the operations people at some of the world's biggest banks, who needed to be inspired by this utopian commercial vision. I could imagine these bankers being not unlike Mr Orange from the ads, preoccupied with their own concerns (banks were not having a good time just then), and would need something to get their imaginations racing, as they were encouraged to picture that world, summed up succinctly in the opening statement. The statement provided the 'Wow' before the 'How' and before the 'Who' of their story, inverting the emphasis of the company's earlier communications. (A useful story format I discuss in more detail later.)

This Wow would transform the bankers' world as much as it would that of the migrant worker in sub-Saharan Africa who would no longer have to walk a whole day to the nearest large town with a bank to collect his wages, or send money home. By envisaging this new future in terms of this individual story, the more epic story of money's next incarnation could inspire the masters of commerce to multiply such examples a billion fold, and imagine their own motivating futures as part of this transactional revolution. Story, singular, selective, focused on a core idea or transformational benefit, can simplify any complexity if you push hard enough and have the courage to pursue radical simplification. Think 'Wow' like they do in movie land, and you can develop a coherent narrative explaining the How and the Who of your story.

Which brings me to the next essential 'C' of storytelling.

# Coherence

So, you have your central idea, the core theme of your story. It stands out clearly, sums you up succinctly, and helps you stand apart from your competitors. Grabbing the attention is one thing, keeping it is quite another. In the worlds of fiction and film this is what separates the blockbusters from the not even off the blocks. But before I get carried away, and promise to impart the sensational secrets of page-turning best-sellerdom (let's face it, if I knew how to write one of those books you wouldn't be holding this one), I'll explain the more humble business of narrative coherence. They're effectively the same thing. Coherence is what makes a story 'a Story', rather than a jumble of ideas, events, images or dialogue.

The dictionary defines coherence as being: "when the parts of something fit together in a natural or sensible way". And it gives us an example: *"There was no coherence between the first and the second half of the film"*.

It's all about making sense, adding up. The right things in the right, logical order. The human mind instinctively seeks pattern. According to Brian Boyd, whose *On the Origin of Stories* offers a 'biocultural' theory of narrative, this tendency is one of the ways storytelling has advanced the evolution of our species. Pattern helped us survive, identifying cyclical rhythms that allowed us to plan for or pursue subsistence. Recognising pattern also alerts us to deviations from the norm, and so attend to potential threats. A vigilant species is a species that survives. Stories similarly reward our attention, developing in us an acute preference for the cognitive behaviours that enabled our species to survive. Both logic and narrative put these needs to work, as the mind incessantly seeks coherent order out of potential chaos.

I've touched on this need already when I argued that telling a coherent story is a far more effective way of demonstrating integrity than simply listing the word as a value. There's a vital relationship operating here, showing how what's essential to the business of storytelling is also vital for the business story. For a novel or film to be successful it must stick to the plot. So must a corporate brand, and the story that brings this to life. Lose the plot and you lose the audience. Lose the audience and you lose their business. They don't walk away from the cinema disappointed, they walk away from your website, brochure, annual report, new business meeting or presentation with the sense that it just didn't add up. Even if they are not sure why, they remain unconvinced.

Plot is an interesting word that reveals a lot about how stories are a reflection of how we see and explain our world. Plot has many dimensions, spatial, organisational and directional. A plot of land is a territory marked out to claim ownership. It's all about potential. The starting point of a building project or venture. Which is where its other main meaning used as a verb comes in. To plot is also to plan, to devise a well-thought out scheme to achieve a specific aim. It is this meaning that is transferred to the craft of narrative. A fictional plot is a similarly well-thought out plan for moving the action forward to a satisfying end. Plotting involves the coherent weaving together of character and incident to arrive at this destination plausibly and enthrallingly.

The plot is thus the structural framework upon which the drama hangs. If it holds up (because it has integrity) so does the story. There will be a logical and aesthetic pleasure in how everything contrives to bring about a satisfying ending. It's not just about the destination itself, but the journey too. The journey is actually the point and pleasure of the narrative. The main characters will remain true to what we know about them throughout. Even if they have magical or superhuman powers we know their limitations (logic and reason still reign in the most irrational fanciful realms). Characters never acquire new powers without an explanation. They don't change their characters without us knowing why. Scrooge changes completely, but that is the whole point of the story. We know why he changes. The Jack Nicholson character in *The Shining* goes off the rails and on the rampage, but we see this developing. His losing the plot is the plot. The fact that we use the phrase 'lost the plot' for someone who no longer makes sense to us, shows how integral our sense of narrative order is in the logic of our lives. Coherence is making sense; sense is made by being coherent in how you present this.

Corporate as much as individual identity needs to stick to the plot. That's true integrity for you.

Brands have their plots too, and need to stick to them. They mark out their territory in the marketplace, a space they can uniquely 'own'. Or, better still, in the consumer's mind: making brand, according to adman John Hegarty, "the most valuable real estate in the world" in owning a corner of this space. We call this ownership a brand's 'positioning', but it could just as easily be called its 'plot'. The brand's 'plot' (space) will be robust, identifiable and defendable. As will the second (planning) sense of the term. A positioning

should have a strategic dimension, a plot for taking the business forward, in pursuit of some future goal. This strategic plot, like its dramatic or fictional counterparts, must be robust, well-thought-through, logical, credible, realistic. In short, coherent. A coherent brand story helps ensure that brand can go the distance.

From the earliest days, stories have involved journeys. The two are so intrinsically linked we can suspect there is some deep functional relationship connecting them buried in prehistory. The prevalence of journey narratives in the earliest myths and epics surely resounds deeply from the migrant soul of our pre-urban ancestors. The urge for going was a vital necessity for hunter-gatherers, and you can imagine dreams of happy hunting grounds just over the horizon forming the staple of the stories they shared to spur each other on. Or when they settled in agricultural communities, how these epic journeys of the past formed a legendary legacy handed down to the now literate urban cultures that followed. Indeed, a very concrete link between storying and journeying survives in the tradition of Australian aboriginal 'Song Lines'. Here 'maps' are oral and memorial, formed of words rather than images, preserving topographical memory and allowing vast distances to be navigated, through the recital of songs recalling mythical footprints across these sacred spaces.

This urge for going must be buried deep in our collective psyche, for it stirs us still. It might partly explain our desire for the vicarious journeys stories take us on, and why stories are tailor-made for narrating and inspiring momentum. Stories take us places, or hold out to us the promise of forward movement, or a goal to be accomplished. The happy hunting grounds or lands of milk and honey the earliest narratives evoked, are still the dominant narratives of most corporate stories. Greater value is always found just over the horizon.

So many stories involve journeys because at their core is a clear goal, a destination the narrative itself is focused on reaching and realising. Homer's Odysseus is the archetypal questor. His *Odyssey* to return home again after the Trojan War set the pattern for journey narratives in the West. Even if the journey is metaphorical, the hero's journey to find him or herself, the goal, the Grail, the promise is the end that brings the story into being. The land of milk and honey (The Bible), Kansas (*The Wizard of Oz*), America itself (*Easy Rider, On the Road*), Enlightenment (*Zen and the Art of Motorcycle Maintenance*); stories have goals, goals create desires, and stories fuel/fulfil those desires through the forward momentum of narrative.

Novelists and screenwriters talk about a work's 'throughline'. This is the thread that binds the narrative and sustains the audience's interest. The throughline is usually the focus of the hero, where he or she wants to be, and everything in the narrative should be in pursuit of this goal. The story involves digressions, diversions and must involve challenges. In fact 'conflict' is the very essence of entertainment stories in any genre, demanding inventive ways to inhibit and challenge the hero's progress towards his or her goal. These challenges create the conflict upon which drama thrives. Yet through all these diversions and challenges, the thread of the hero's objective has to be clear, focused and followed. The need for clarity and the need for coherence meet at this point. Coherence, through the means of a 'throughline', is clarity in action.

Focus, thread and momentum are also essential in commercial communications. If your brand promises something (and it should), then there is an implied momentum, and journeying built into the offer. If it solves a problem (and it should), then it demonstrates how it can help overcome the challenges its audiences face. Your promise is the destination of the journey on which you will take your audiences. Until they accompany you on that real journey, they only have your 'plot' (plan, strategic intent) to go on. Your story is thus the surrogate for the journey on which you promise to take people. It gratifies the urge for going and forward momentum, by holding up a promise, and offering a clear thread for getting there. And it should inspire trust that you can take them there by the coherence and integrity of this thread. A coherent fictional plot delivers a satisfying story with a satisfying resolution. A narrative problem solved. A coherent business story also sticks to the plot, holds together, adds up, and so inspires trust that you will also deliver a satisfying resolution. A business problem solved.

But novels and films do more than make sense, satisfying the brain's instinctive need for logical order. They excite – pinning audiences to the edges of their seats, or making them miss tube stops or beauty sleep because they simply "couldn't put it down". Page-turning magic is Coherence Plus. Plus what? And can any of this magic be transferred to the business of corporate communications? Yes. The business story can learn from the story business even here. For brands and their stories don't just have to make sense, inspiring trust through logical and narrative integrity. They have to make you want them. They have to be compelling. Relationships are built on trust, but driven by desire, and desire is what the master storytellers build into their well-constructed, page-turning narratives. If coherence provides the essential thread of a narrative, this is the golden strand woven into that thread. Binding the audience close, and making the master weavers of the story guild very rich indeed.

Entertainment stories exist entirely to gratify the desire to know 'what happens next?' It's like a drug, and can be very powerful, rewarding the attention afforded the narrative with serial doses of neurochemical stimulation. What has any of this to do with the sober business of corporate communications? The business equivalent of 'what happens next' is 'what's in it for me?'. Not the gratification of curiosity as a thrilling end in itself, but the fulfilment of a need the story is founded upon. The ultimate point of any commercial communication is the call to action. 'Get in touch'; 'find out more…'. How often we see or use that phrase, unconsciously announcing the premise of storytelling in the day-to-day functionality and rhetoric of communications practice. The desire to know more was what kept Scheherazade alive in *A Thousand and One Nights* through the spell of narrative. Story kept her alive, and it can keep a business or brand relationship alive, by making your offer, expressed through story, as compelling as possible.

Want to know how? Then read on…

# Emotional connection

Storytelling has thus far been a craft, perhaps even a science, whose principles can be applied systematically to deliver predictable ends. My metaphors have all been physical, deriving from the hard-edged world of things and their relationships. Until now this communications vehicle has been travelling mostly on the left-hand side of the brain. Calculatedly, as I have set out to convince the world of Business, which is more comfortable dwelling in these regions, of the benefits of story to deliver its messages and achieve its goals. It is now time to cross the tracks. Leaving the hard, sharp world of systems and structures for the softer, fuzzy world of feelings and imagination. The kind of stuff that might make story unwelcome on Planet Business, raising its Vulcan eyebrows at its 'illogical' nature. But story is perfectly logical. Combining both the rational with the emotional to deliver what might be called the logic of the heart. A logic perfectly fitted to the way most humans think, feel and act.

Whatever we might like to believe, most decisions we make are influenced by emotions rather than reason. Especially the Big Ones. A house is probably the biggest financial transaction most of us will make outside of business hours. A spouse is probably the most significant legally-binding relationship we are ever likely to form. Yet both life-changing transactions are taken with something other than our heads in the driving seat. Our heads may have done the groundwork (I speak only of property searches here), but ultimately it's the heart or the 'gut' – our emotions – that carry the day. We readily admit to this. That we "just knew" he or she was "the one". Or that the house "chose me", rather than vice versa. The bigger the deal, the more inclined we are to trust our emotions in brokering it. Why should it be so very different in the world of business, where (financial) stakes are even higher, and relationships (almost) as important for long-term stability, happiness and success?

And yet the most valuable currency of the business world, trust, is minted purely out of emotions. I can tell you to trust me. I can ask you to trust me, and provide lots of rational arguments for why you should. Yet the more I insist on this, the less likely it is you will comply. As with the houses or spouses you didn't choose, if it doesn't feel right, it isn't right, and our relationship just isn't going anywhere. You can grow to trust me through experience, if I reliably deliver on my promises. But until then all you have to go on is the information I give out, and I don't mean facts, details and raw data. Not just what I say, but also how I say it. My body language, if we meet in person; or how I communicate through language, look, feel, imagery, and tone of voice, if you are relying on the communications that stand in for me. The story I tell. Story, the whole-brain vehicle of communication, again serves as a surrogate for the relationship I hope to build with you. Unashamedly embracing emotion, story plays a vital role in business communications, building the connections through which trust just might flow.

Emotional Connection is therefore the final vital ingredient for storytelling. Quite literally vital, in that it is by connecting emotionally that stories bring communications to life. Without emotion you don't really have a story. Or if you do, it's only doing half of its job or fulfilling half of its potential to move or influence people. A focused, logically-ordered string of ideas or statements is not much more than a sterile list without emotional connection. And connection is what stories do best. "Only connect" was the novelist E. M. Forster's rallying cry:"Only connect the prose and the passion, and both will be exalted. And human love will be seen at its height. Live in fragments no longer. Only connect..." His prescription for a fulfilled life applies equally to his chosen craft. Making connections is what fiction does best. Connecting sentences together into fluid narrative prose. But also connecting what he termed the "passion" with the "prose". The prose of everyday life, with the passion of authentic emotion enshrined in great art. Not just the relationship between things – science, engineering, architecture can do all this – but the vital connection stories can forge between the storyteller and his or her audience.

Stories help us relate; in all senses of the word. Relate means to tell. To report on an event or series of events that have already happened. It's quite a cold, cerebral, no-nonsense word in this sense. Very business like. A witness relates what he or she saw in a court of law.

But 'relate' also means to form a connection. To see eye-to-eye, to understand one another. If you relate *with* me, rather than just to me, we are on the same wavelength, sharing a tacit understanding that is in itself a form of communication. It may not even involve words, perhaps looks, gestures, unconscious signals; but this form of relate is far more powerful than the first kind. Relate in this way and we have a relationship, an emotional bond that can nurture trust. We trust people we relate to, and trust what they relate to us. We are more likely to trust a piece of gossip than a piece of advertising. Why? Principally because the people we gossip with are on our wavelength. We relate to them, therefore we are more likely to take in and pass on what they have told us.

So, how do you make your story 'relate' in this enriched sense? Again, by learning from the Classics. They have remained relevant because they deal with universal human truths, going straight to the heart of life. The themes they touch on – freedom, friendship, ambition, enlightenment, heroism, belonging, discovery, sacrifice, love – touch us deeply, appealing to a central emotional core. Emotional connection with a character is actually the real driver of narrative interest. Without it you don't have a centre of attention and identification. If the audience doesn't care about or relate to the hero, it won't care what happens next to him or her, no matter how cleverly the plot is constructed. Emotional connection moves people to turn the page.

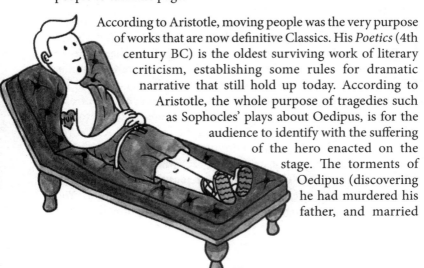

According to Aristotle, moving people was the very purpose of works that are now definitive Classics. His *Poetics* (4th century BC) is the oldest surviving work of literary criticism, establishing some rules for dramatic narrative that still hold up today. According to Aristotle, the whole purpose of tragedies such as Sophocles' plays about Oedipus, is for the audience to identify with the suffering of the hero enacted on the stage. The torments of Oedipus (discovering he had murdered his father, and married his mother to name but a few), were designed to arouse pity and terror in the audience. These emotions, Aristotle theorised, actually had a positive, cleansing effect on the audience. A form of group therapy, through the empathetic power of dramatic art.

Empathy is instinctive in humans and certain animals, with humans able to mirror the emotions of adults from within an hour of birth. We just can't help it, feeling with the emotions we see enacted in art as if we were actually experiencing them, and projecting our own emotions and sentiments on to others. The supposed emotional cleansing such empathy affords is where the idea of 'Catharsis' comes from, which Freud used (along with the plot of Oedipus) for the storytelling therapy he promoted as a science. By telling their own stories, re-enacting their own traumatic dramas, Freud's patients would be similarly cleansed of negative emotions. Stories, as thinkers both ancient and modern have recognised, have a unique emotive potency that operates beyond the literary stage or page.

Now, this is not to suggest that your corporate story should be modelled on a Greek tragedy, or even that it need take on Epic proportions. Quite the opposite, in fact. What we learn from the Classics is not their grandeur, but their humility. Oedipus was a king, but the members of the audience were not, nor were Freud's patients. The Classics touch us because they have basic human emotions at their core. They transcend history, nationality, class and context, through this universal human appeal. For all their fancy dress and grandeur, they keep it real. Crown on head, but feet on ground, because the human heart beats loudly throughout. As Robert McKee explains, applying this principle to cinema: "we go to the movies to enter a new, fascinating world, to inhabit vicariously another human being who at first seems so unlike us, and yet at heart is like us... We do not wish to escape life but to find life, to use our minds in fresh, experimental ways, to flex our emotions, to enjoy, to learn, to add depth to our days". No matter how fantastic their wrappers, at the core a story needs to touch us on this universal level. Far from being about escapism, they must involve the recognitions and relevance McKee describes. The Classics remain relevant because they deal with emotional realities that affect us and touch us still today. You don't need to write a Classic, but you need to keep it real, keep it relevant, make it human. Only connect.

It was in a small back room up a narrow flight of stairs in Hammersmith, one dreary Tuesday evening a few years ago. There were about nine of us, crammed into the space, surrounded by depleted party-platters and un-drunk wine in plastic cups. All of us intensely focused on what the people were saying and doing on the other side of a two-way mirror directly in front of us. This time it was a focus group of seasoned smokers who were considering quitting their habit. We were researching creative concepts for materials promoting NHS services to help smokers quit. We'd mocked-up the front covers of some leaflets that might appear in a doctor's waiting room or a pharmacy, providing information and guidance on how the NHS could help. There were a couple of different routes, and one, as ever, we the agency preferred.

It was this route's turn. And as the boards were handed round, the group suddenly opened up and came to life, excitedly discussing as one body the images and headlines we had put together. They weren't assessing the merits of the creative. They were telling stories about what they saw.

Each mocked-up leaflet featured a photograph of an individual depicted in a real situation looking directly at the viewer. There was a short quotation about issues relevant to quitting, but in the voice of the smoker or ex-smoker. Yet, on the basis of one image and at the most ten words, the group were busily speculating on the lives of these characters. One image – depicting a twinkly-eyed senior citizen emerging from a swimming pool – had participants discussing the new life they imagined she must be now enjoying. "She's probably doing a lot more other things now, too", one said. "Seeing her grandchildren, getting out more". When asked why this route scored such a hit, respondents said these pieces spoke to them in their language, showed people with whom they could identify, didn't lecture them about their habit, but made them believe they too could actually quit. It was like hearing the client's brief read back to us from the mouths of the target audience That's about as good as it gets in this game.

The project was to re-design the look and feel, and messaging for the Department of Health's 'Smokefree' campaign, promoting NHS Stop Smoking Services. Smokefree had been launched in 2006 to publicise the ban on smoking in public places. The brand then evolved to promote the public services available to smokers. The literature also offered information and advice about products on the market, and different methods for quitting. There was lots of information, plenty of scary medical facts, but also inspirational imagery intended to capture the spirit of a smoke-free world. Lots of blue skies and happy people living the full rich healthy life.

There was plenty of emotion therefore to sugar the advice pill, but this was found to be a bit too abstract and remote from the lives of the hardened smokers these services most needed to reach. The Smokefree brand needed to get real if it was going to connect with real people, real smokers, and inspire them to quit. Which is how we found ourselves watching a focus group confirming we had done just that. And so we made getting real, through imagery, tone of voice and attitude, the new touchstone for the brand. But what I hadn't quite realised when writing the original headlines, was that what we were really doing was telling stories, and how powerful this could be to make human connections through identification.

By making this connection these mini narratives drew people in, and because they showed we understood them, they were more ready to trust the information the publications contained. Getting real was really about telling stories, and, like they do on soap operas, engaging audiences in dramas around real issues that were personally relevant brought to life by characters with whom they could relate.

A smoker-filled room in Hammersmith is an unlikely setting for an epiphany, but it was here that I conclusively discovered the emotive power of story as a communications tool.

# *Making the connection*

Emotional connection is as important to corporate as it is to consumer communications, ultimately overriding such distinctions by appealing to human nature. Whatever business you are in, and however virtual the conversation, people buy from people. Stories help those people connect, and by connecting do business. Your head of Investor Relations or CFO may have no time for such fluffy stuff as stories, or much time for considering the human side of who you are and what you do. They may assert that: "the facts speak for themselves". Facts don't speak. People do. And they speak to other people. Drive emotion out of your story and you are only appealing to half the brains of your audience, standing less chance of being preferred, loved or remembered.

Too many businesses speak like businesses to other businesses. As if the fiction of business-to-business communications was a reality. As if these abstractions and legal functions we have created really could speak to one another, like mainframes conversing without the need for human beings. Until that happens, it is better that people communicate with people. By recognising a shared humanity, engaging the emotions and imagination as well as the intellect, we more effectively make the connections upon which business, indeed all human commerce and communication, depends. Have always depended. Story recognises and relates to the caveman clad in pinstripe. The semi-rational being making important decisions often involving vast amounts of money, but employing the same cognitive equipment given to our skin-clad ancestors. The more complex the world and the way we access it becomes, the more useful it is to remember this, and rely on the tools that have assisted us for millennia.

Well, that's the theory. Yet every year Radley Yeldar conducts a best practice survey called *What's the Story* measuring how well the FTSE 100 companies manage to articulate their story across key communications. The short and rather dispiriting answer is, "not very". They can relate – facts, figures, statistics – but they don't relate with anyone. 'Leading' is the main message and favourite claim of the majority of companies, regardless of sector. Yes, we know you are large and leading, that's why you're a FTSE 100 company. They make grandiose epic statements – World's largest producer of (something); Mexico's second-largest … (Mexican?). Or frankly meaningless ones, such as my personal favourite: "The world's third-largest primary platinum producer". But too often lose sight of the humanity that would make their story relevant. Size and scale may mean a lot to you, but they remove you conclusively from the human realm you are there to serve. No matter how distant what you do is from the day-to-day, you are still part of a chain that ultimately touches people and serves human needs. The further up that chain you are, the more important it is to ensure your story makes clear how you touch people's lives, and *why* this matters.

I'll briefly reference a few examples (both good and bad) from Radley Yeldar's research.

For some businesses or sectors, making an emotional connection is far easier; as what they do is intrinsically and directly connected with the human. Not surprisingly, pharmaceutical companies are generally quite good at this. The preservation of human life is certainly a strong foundation for telling a compelling story to which we can immediately relate. Whatever scepticism might haunt our rational view of the pharma sector's operations and motivations, we know why it is there and why this ultimately matters.

Shire is a shining example of this. It has a great line about its business, which aspires to be: "As brave as the people we help". Some people find this a bit schmaltzy, but what's nice is the way it puts a common humanity at the core of its offer, making a clear connection between why the company exists, and how it goes about things. Bravery is put forward as a principle of how it claims to take on its own business challenges. This, at the very least, attempts to build empathy between the business and its customers.

But you don't have to save lives to make emotional connections. Diageo, who own a lot of alcoholic drink brands, usually does quite well in the survey. As a classic 'house of brands' it would be easy for it to hang back, and let its brands do all the talking and make all the friends. Yet it still manages to personalise its relationship to these brands by personifying itself as a 'custodian' of the heritage of brands like Guinness. Its focus is on "Celebrating life, every day, everywhere". Even custodians can let their hair down occasionally, and join the party its brands help to go with a swing.

Nor do you have to sell exciting products to make clear how you touch people's lives. G4S is a business-to-business security company. And whilst it starts off with the usual strutting and puffing – "the world's leading international security solutions group" – it at least explains what all this bigness amounts to. Which is: safeguarding "the welfare and prosperity of millions of people worldwide – helping to create safer and better environments in which people live and work". It then paints a picture of how this story unfolds in the world we all inhabit:

"We protect rock stars and sports stars, people and property, including some of the world's most important buildings and events.

From advising on stadium building plans to crowd control and ensuring event tickets are not forged;

From delivering pay packets to ensuring ATMs have enough cash to meet your shopping needs;

From delivering cash to bank branches and retail outlets to managing the flow of cash for central banks and major retailers;

From ensuring travellers have a safe and pleasant experience in ports and airports around the world to secure detention and escorting of people who are not lawfully entitled to remain in a country;

In more ways than you might realise, G4S is securing your world."

It's not the world's greatest story by a long chalk (and I even excised a bit about risk assessment, and "integrated solutions" where they sounded like everyone else). But it has a clear theme, and a coherent thread; and once they get into their stride this does paint a picture that just about anyone can recognise. We've got rock stars and cash points, criminals and exotic voyages. The stuff dreams are made on, and the stuff every day is. All contribute to an imaginative 'mural' that comes to life in our imaginations through word-painting, bringing an otherwise anonymous company into much more colourful focus. It is a Business-to-Business company, yet by talking about "your world", it acknowledges that its audiences all exist in the same one; and that what G4S ultimately delivers – security – benefits that world in numerous ways.

Any business or sector can make the emotional connection if they put their minds (or hearts) to it. By remembering the human need they serve and the human audience they are presumably addressing. Yet every year the survey reveals companies who have the potential for an emotionally rich and compelling story handed to them on a plate. But they completely fail to serve it up. I'll finally reference an extreme, but by no means atypical, example of such missed opportunities.

Of all the sectors, retail touches us most directly every day. Of all the sub-sets of the sector, fashion is about the sexiest. Of all the UK fashion brands Burberry is among the most iconic, has a rich and unique heritage, and therefore all the ingredients of a compelling corporate story. And yet the face Burberry Group plc shows to the world, couldn't be more different from the one seductively pouting at us from the main Burberry site. From the catwalk to the counting house is a matter of one click; but by visiting the 'Investors' pages we enter an entirely different world. The brand name is the same, and there is still a smattering of glamorous images, but the entire personality has changed. Here is a representative gobbet from the 'Our Strategy' pages at time of writing (July 2012):

"An ongoing focus on replenishment capability and practices saw the penetration of replenishment styles remain at about half of mainline revenue. Assortment planning and execution was further improved. A more consistent global buy provided increased supply chain efficiency and a cohesive brand statement across the store base, whilst allowing regional flexibility to respond to local preferences".

Can this really be the same business that deals in such seductive dreams and desires? The Burberry 'business' brand is deliberately estranged from its sexy consumer-facing sibling. So concerned is it about being taken seriously by the investor community it performs a kind of reverse alchemy in the story it tells them.

The Burberry fashion brand confers a magical allure to textile commodities, through uniquely ownable trademarks and the meanings they have come to confer. This allows the company to charge exponentially higher prices than the intrinsic worth of those garments, and these margins in turn contribute directly to revenues, operating profits and shareholder returns. This is the Burberry business story stated plainly. A story of alchemy. The Burberry brand turns humble wool, silk, cotton, ethanol plus vegetable extracts into pure gold. And yet the Burberry business brand reverses this alchemy; turning the glamour and allure it trades in into a verbal commodity, cut from the generic broadcloth of collective business speak. And whilst Burberry "continued to focus on customer service, driving consistency and productivity by better connecting with customers and cultivating personalised relationships", it neglects to do the same with this other important audience. Making money and talking about it, appear to be an entirely different matter.

As I've said, this is not atypical of how many businesses speak to their business and investor audiences. Burberry is singled out here simply because of the extraordinary disparity between the face of the consumer brand, and that of Burberry Group plc . Such differences are deeply problematic for a number of reasons, and ultimately self-defeating for the purposes of investor relations, which function to inspire trust.

Jargon dehumanises, disengages, and disguises the authentic self of a business or brand. It might be adopted to inspire trust – believing it encourages a collective tribal identification through shared linguistic codes – but ultimately it does the opposite. The whole point of any communications within a competitive context is to put across a distinctive, even unique offer. This enables people to understand who you authentically are, and so feel more inclined to do business with or invest in you, instead of another. It's harder to do that if you sound like everyone else. Even unconsciously people might wonder why you have adopted a borrowed cloak. What is it you are hiding? Even the simple matter of using the first person plural 'we', or the active voice, rather than 'the business' or a passive construction, can help humanise the story. The passive might sound more formal – "gradual improvements were made in the operating profits" – yet it doesn't suggest you are actually in control. The more 'public' the language, the harder it is for individuals to relate to it, and ultimately to the people who stand behind it. Don't stand behind it, stand in front of it. How can you expect anyone to trust you if they can't look you in the eye?

And how can they trust you if you tell different stories to different audiences? Imagine all the audiences you need to talk to assembled in one room. Could you tell them one single story about your business? Why not? It's a provocative, but increasingly relevant, question. By attempting to be different things to different people you end up being nothing to anyone. Or worse. The more fragmented your story, the less integrity this suggests, the less trust you are likely to inspire. A hero doesn't change his or her identity halfway through a story. Nor should you. If you tell conflicting stories, rather than different expressions of a single, credible, provable narrative, then you inspire little faith in there being much substance to your tale. Whether you invite them into a single room or not, the likes of social media, social enterprise and social responsibility are making everything visible, and audience segregation nearly impossible. The walls are coming down. Communications is going open plan.

# The Middle

"The object of art is to give life a shape"
William Shakespeare,
*A Midsummer Night's Dream*

chapter three
# How to Develop your Story

—

They say everyone's got a novel inside them. I'm not so sure. I've worked in publishing, and seen Reject Manuscript Mountain. It's a depressing sight. If there really is a novel in everyone, not everyone has what it takes to get it out and share it with the world. Robert McKee has called story "the hardest thing we all do". The good news is, because we all 'do' story, we are all instinctively experts in what makes a well-told tale. We just have to remember and embrace this in the business context. And so, whilst not everyone has a publishable novel or blockbuster screenplay in them, every business has a story to tell. If you truly know your business you can tell your story. You don't have to create a work of art, but you can learn from them – applying what works in the story business to your business story.

# The quest for your story

Cinema again provides the most useful model for doing this. You could say cinema has perfected the fine art of narrative compulsion for commercial ends. And whilst commerciality probably smothers too much creativity at birth, the industry still manages to tell stories that make sense and move people. These stories work because they tend to draw repeatedly on archetypes that have served the industry since its infancy. Some of these classic plots go back to the very origins of storytelling, yet remain useful, relevant and bankable today. Hollywood continues to find a market for its products not because they are perennially new, but reassuringly old. Or as Jonah Sachs recently put it, perfectly summing up the power of mythic narratives in any context:

"These tales are deeply ingrained in our DNA, and no matter where or when you were born, certain patterns of stories will influence you enormously. When we hear stories based on these patterns, we feel more like we're remembering something forgotten than learning something new".

Not every new film is a Classic, but the ones that work tend to be based on them at some level. Pouring new wine into very old bottles for successive generations.

This archetypal emphasis should reassure and embolden any company tempted to despair that it might not have anything 'original' to say as the makings of its story. If a multi-billion-dollar industry can repeatedly riffle through the Seven Basic Plots and still find infinite capacity for invention; if the human taste for heroics can connect across the centuries that divide *Beowulf* (the Anglo-Saxon epic poem, not the 2007 movie), and *Wolverine III* (which I assume is either in production or out already by the time you read this), then any company who trusts in the power and techniques of storytelling can share its own tale with the world.

Of all the identifiable archetypes perhaps the most universal, and most relevant for our purposes, is the quest narrative. Nearly every epic falls into this category, from the Babylonian *Epic of Gilgamesh* to *Lord of The Rings*, via *Pilgrim's Progress*, to James Joyce's *Ulysses* and *O Brother Where Art Thou* (both based on Homer's *Odyssey*). This is Joseph Campbell's *Hero With A Thousand Faces*, constituting what he called the 'monomyth' of the hero's journey. As Campbell describes it in his introduction:

"A hero ventures forth from the world of common day into a region of supernatural wonder: fabulous forces are there encountered and a decisive victory is won: the hero comes back from this mysterious adventure with the power to bestow boons on his fellow man."

Campbell claimed this myth was identifiable in the stories of Christ and The Buddha, as well as Homer's Odysseus, and has subsequently inspired that of Luke Skywalker. Quest narratives reveal the close relationship between stories and journeys, as they follow the hero's journeying to find some Grail, but ultimately to find him or herself. Some quest narratives only involve metaphorical journeys, with the questor journeying into him or herself to find enlightenment or discover their true identity. And whilst this might appear to be stretching a point for the purposes of artistic classification, it does show the robust flexibility of its basic structure, and how it might prove useful as a working model for developing a core corporate narrative. Or, to put it another way, you don't have to be in the travel business to find the journey archetype useful here.

That's the power of archetypes. They are applicable anywhere. Their universality allows us to look beyond the local details of what a business actually does, to identify a core truth that might form the basis of a story. The hero may be dressed in armour, bearing the shield of Arthurian allegiance, or in uniform wearing the badge of LAPD; but he or she is setting out to find something. These heroes find themselves a whole lot wiser at the end, and we the audience journey with them, share in the wisdom they gain and imaginatively apply it to our own desires and circumstances. That's why quests and journeys provide the perfect models for our purposes. They have knowledge, experience and momentum locked into their very structure. For as George Clooney's character in *O Brother* keeps saying, "Everybody's looking for answers". And every company has a yearning desire to get 'somewhere', to get on. Stagnation is as destructive to business as it is to dramatic fiction. Your story is the surrogate for the journey of discovery and fulfilment you promise. If the story inspires, coheres and compels, then customers will be inclined to embark on that journey with you.

## *Scripting a core story*

We often use the following exercise at workshops, helping clients develop their own core story by looking to Hollywood. The session adapts a version of the classic story arc structure employed in countless movies. Comprising:

1. Introducing the hero's world

2. The quest identified

3. The journey, involving trials and challenges

4. The resolution: the hero's transformed world is re-established.

You can identify this structure underlying the majority of Hollywood movies, adapting a basic outline that has served storytellers since at least the days of Aristotle.

What follows is an overview of a half-day story development workshop. It's designed to provide a starting point for thinking about using the discipline of creative story development to define a company's brand offer. I should point out that, although I'm drawing on an archetypal pattern made visible in countless Hollywood treatments, this doesn't involve applying Archetypal Psychology to the business of brand building. That's a whole different discipline, beyond the scope of this discussion, and more readily applicable to consumer product branding. Whilst a product brand can usefully model itself on a human type – be these Rebels, Sages, or Jesters – so that it resonates at a deep unconscious level with consumers, a company is already crammed full of human beings. Their collective history, culture, values, ambitions and energies contribute to who it uniquely is, or could be. A product brand can be whatever it needs to be, based on opportunity or perceived need, a corporate brand needs to enter into dynamic dialogue between who it is and who it wants to be. If archetypes are used they need to be reflections of an authentic reality, defined by culture; rather than entirely projections of an ideal self.

The workshop methodology is designed for companies who want to discover or re-discover their core stories. It might be used as part of a brand development process (with the due diligence of interviews, audits, consultation and visual development all playing their allotted roles). Story, as I've suggested, is often a more acceptable term than brand in some places. And so using a story development workshop for a specific communications task might open new horizons for the company and its brand. The journey we are about to go on may be the start of a bigger journey still.

# the hero's world

Every fictional story starts by introducing the hero and the world in which he or she lives. This establishes the normality that will soon be disrupted by the events of the narrative. A story needs a hero, and it is also useful to think about any brand or business in heroic terms. For a start it encourages singularity of focus. Even superheroes can't be all things to all people, or they risk being bland or confusing.

In a start up or less-established company the hero is likely to resemble the founders. They are the story as it currently stands, but what heroic qualities are they blessed with? In what way are they going to change the world? A charismatic CEO might be the media face of the company, and the first PR reference point. But can the company's story really be carried on one man or woman's shoulders? The limitations of that are obvious, given the average churn at the top. It's unwise to put all your egos in one basket when seeking to develop a sustainable story. Branson is Branson, but we also know what he stands for, and how this runs through every venture Virgin embarks on. And so, whilst it's useful to imagine an individual 'hero' when thinking about the company's story, this is largely an analogy. A corporate brand should be *like* an individual, but not exclusively embodied in one.

Thinking of your brand as a hero, and taking him or her on the classic journey of self-discovery encourages us to get to the heart of your offer, the motivating Why it ultimately matters. This heroic structure helps identify the big idea at the heart of your brand, which allows you to develop its story. We start by taking stock of our hero's world in the here and now. Covering the following broad themes:

Where have you come from?

Who is important to you?

What do you value?

Who do you compete with?

What presents a threat to your world?

What do people say about you?

Some of these questions will be more relevant than others, and some will prove more difficult to tease out or gain agreement on. It's useful at this stage to consider a company's heritage, or, in screenwriting parlance the 'back story' to the narrative. Where the hero has come from may play a defining role in his or her identity and motivations. The company's founding vision, the challenges it has already overcome, even its 'family tree' (if it has come about through a whole series of alliances), may be relevant to the story we are now shaping. We may even be chronicling a corporate legend of ancient standing. But a heritage story isn't right for everyone. And as many quest narratives show, back story often holds the hero back. Think of all those flashbacks explaining why a hero suddenly doubts his or her abilities at a crucial moment. It's best to get this all out in the open before we start. Heritage might contribute to who you are, but you need to assess what is useful from the past going forward. You can't take everything with you on your journey. It will only weigh you down.

Who is important to the hero? Will this change, does it need to? Who are the principal beneficiaries of your business, the most important audiences for your story? It is worth identifying them on setting out, as you must be accountable to them later. This means internal stakeholders and audiences as well as external. Is the hero an independent loner, free to define his or her own destiny, or forge fruitful alliances down the road? Or are you part of a family, with a Group of different siblings or brand offspring crowding around? Do they contribute to your story, or hold you back?

If there is a hero there must be an antagonist, or a set of forces determined to thwart his or her progress. After all, it is often the arrival of a threat that encourages the hero to first show heroic properties, and embark on the journey. A common enemy is one of the most powerful means for galvanising any company into defining who it is, and rallying together to oppose it. Knowing who you are not and why – "we just don't do things like that"... X would be quite happy to do that, but we would take a different route" – can be really useful in forming the nub of a story. Knowing who you are is partly knowing who you are not (as the showdowns between the likes of Apple and Microsoft; Coke and Pepsi; Virgin and the World testify).

This threat might not take the form of competitors, but can be found in external forces that compel the hero to put up a fight or take a different course. These might be the circumstances that have encouraged the company to take stock of who it is, and where it needs to go as enshrined in its new story. The story it tells and the story it lives may be the much-needed catalyst to a new future. But these threats may more insidiously and dangerously lurk within. No hero is perfect, else we mortals couldn't identify with him or her. It is the imperfections that the narrative puts to the test. As the hero might have to vanquish his or her own demons to fulfil his or her destiny, so a company may have to come to terms with things that hold it back and prevent it moving forward. These demons – constituting the shadowy counterparts of the hero's own ideal image – might represent the threat of what you will become if you do not embark on your transformative journey. Dealing with these at the set up means they are more easily identified and vanquished when they are encountered later.

Every hero has special qualities, the powers or weapons that will protect him or her, and be sorely tested during the course of adventures. What are yours? What makes you special? This is a common question when defining brands; but putting it in this journey framework helps to focus the mind on whether such qualities are useful or sustainable. Are these the strengths and values that can equip you for the road ahead? These might evolve in response to the journey, or you may need to acquire new ones along the way. The narrative mindset and forward focus involved in developing a story encourage a rigorous examination of values, helping to challenge complacency about the values you might believe are fixed in stone. Will they serve you well on the journey? If not, the questor needs to challenge them.

Finally, what do people say about you? In the press, around the industry, even internally? Are you happy with this, or do you want to be more in control of this reputation, by proving you are able to create a different reality? A useful exercise for drawing this out is to imagine the company's epitaph. What would people say about you if you expired tomorrow? Would it be the sad tale of potential unfulfilled, a life half lived? If so, lament not. There's still time to change all that. The journey hasn't even begun.

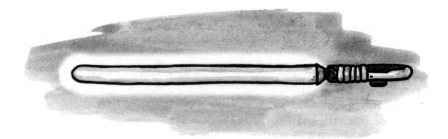

the
uest

Conflict is the essence of drama, and through conflict change. The call to go on a quest brings about that conflict, representing a classic example of what Aristotle – the world's first story theorist – called 'The Inciting Incident'. The well-made Aristotelian drama is usually in three parts, with a beginning, middle and end. The story really starts with this incident, which kick starts the action by presenting a problem to be solved. At their most basic, dramatic narratives are problem-solving mechanisms. You set a problem up in The Inciting Incident, and make your hero solve it (but never easily), through the twists and turns of the narrative. In a quest narrative this initiates the search for whatever is needed to resolve the crisis. And so the journey begins. The hero might not want to go on the journey, and be quite happy with things as they are. But stasis is not an option. If things stayed the same there would be no drama, no story. Even superheroes have to prove themselves occasionally.

Journeys always involve challenges, even sacrifices. What's important now might not always be so. The journey helps us understand and accept that. One of the major advantages of imagining the company as an archetypal hero is the objectivity this affords. An archetype universalises, and so de-personalises sufficiently to allow people to imagine other possible futures freed from the past or politics. As Oscar Wilde put it, "Give [a man] a mask and he will tell you the truth". We're not talking about role playing here (although that can prove useful in places), so much as identifying what's important to our hero on his or her journey. The hero can only retain what's useful to fulfil the quest. And so going along with the logic and momentum demanded by story can help companies let go of some dearly held sacred principles going forward. Going forward is what narrative, and ultimately business is all about.

The identification of a quest, a Grail to aspire to, helps us imagine the different realities the hero could occupy, serving ultimately as a catalyst for change. The quest journey may actually reinforce the need to restore order, or go back to basics, in the face of imposed change. If so, then like the hero in the story, the self-knowledge gained through the quest is invaluable and well worth the journey. Remember, quest journeys usually have a metaphorical dimension (testimony to their deep psychological resonance), with the hero proving he or she has the strength to respond to challenges. Heroes often return from their journeying, and know the place they left for the first time. That's what Dorothy learns from *Oz*, and Gulliver discovers on his *Travels*; understanding either the blessings or shortcomings of the worlds they temporarily left behind.

This exercise can therefore put an existing corporate or brand strategy through its paces, road-testing it through the rigours of the journey undertaken to turn it into a story. We're now deep into the dynamics of storytelling as perfected by the dream-dealers of the silver screen, and so we can give full scope to imaginative inventiveness that defines their ability to touch and move millions. So, the big question posed at this stage is:

What is your vision, your goal, your Grail?

Most companies will have a vision somewhere about the organisation. They may even have a Big Hairy Audacious Goal roaming their corridors, like some Yeti yet to be captured (or accomplished). Identifying the quest for the corporate story provides a good opportunity to dust off the vision or see if the goal is quite as big, hairy and audacious as it needs to be. Thinking in terms of a quest gives the task of defining the focus for the corporate story a singularity and inspirational urgency that might be lacking in an existing vision or goal. The screenwriter or author constantly asks him or herself, what does my protagonist want? This informs the 'throughline', and it should for yours too. The problem with many corporate visions is they tend not to be all that visionary or focused enough. Vision suggests clarity, something you can see, almost touch, it is so distinct and real. We're back to the need for stories to have focus, sharp-edged definition instead of woolly sentiments or rhetoric. Story helps you make your vision visible. When a hero has the vision that sends him or her on their quest there is no ambiguity about the goal. They reach out to touch it, but it dissolves, and so they set out to find it. Realising the vision becomes the goal.

'Grail' might be a more useful term here. Evoking both vision and goal, this romance archetype has entered common parlance as a metaphor for a mission of singular intent. The Grail of your narrative should also be crystal clear, luminous in its tangibility and achievability; but also aspirational and inspirational. Would it allow your story to stand out distinctly enough from your competitors'? Is it precise and lucid in its details, but also missionary enough to motivate people to pursue it, and transform your business story? The story of a business transformed. It's useful to really picture this changed reality before setting out, and question whether you have what it takes for achieving it now, or whether you are prepared to change. If your existing corporate vision or goal has these qualities, then they can contribute to the Grail of your narrative. If not, then push harder before setting out. No conflict, no drama, no story.

I'm not suggesting you now have to put 'Grail' alongside vision and BHAG on the shelf of things you ought to have or need to say. Rather, by applying the rigours demanded of well-made narrative, you can bring greater clarity, coherence and momentum to that strategy. Story puts strategy to the test. Its role is to distil strategic thinking – demanding a streamlined singularity of focus that has no room for woolly (or even hairy) thinking. The quest for your Grail is simply a means to an end here. It helps to road-test the robustness and usefulness of any existing strategic thinking, by exploring whether it stands up or stands out strongly enough to be the basis of your story. If you can imagine your future in terms of a clear and compelling story, then it is more likely to be realisable. Trial by narrative, if you will, tested by the rigours and disciplines of the journey.

# the ourney

The Grail identified, this becomes the inspirational focus of the story you are developing, and the 'throughline' of the narrative you start to plot out. It's now time to put it and your own heroic mettle to the test. The hero often comes to a crossroads soon after setting out, and faces the first challenge to his or her resolve. You also need to be absolutely certain of the direction you propose taking with your story before you develop it much further. Start by questioning the Grail itself, put the proposed theme and focus of your story on trial. Literally, if it helps. Elect some devil's advocates to question the proposed direction. There are bound to be a few sceptics in the group anyway, so dragoon them into defending it. Make its firmest advocates the ones who pull it apart.

Start with the big question: '*Who cares* if this is the theme and focus of your story?' Is it compelling, differentiating, motivating? Will it make a difference to anyone? Especially those who matter most to you. This might even involve some role playing (as we are now in full dramatic flight), with people representing the perspectives of various stakeholder groups. The audiences identified at the outset can now raise some challenges, repeatedly questioning '*What's in it for me?*' This helps to ensure your road trip doesn't turn into an ego trip. The story you tell, the direction you take, needs to be compelling for those that matter most to you. If not, take another path. It's better to go back to the drawing board than to head off in the wrong direction, and end up in Vanity Fair or even the Slough of Despond.

The dramatic insistence of conflict as the essence of narrative finds its counterpart in the need to identify a real problem to solve. The need you fulfil, the difference you make, should have an urgency and relevance to it. If not, it probably doesn't have the makings of a compelling story, nor a very compelling brand offer. How urgent will depend on the sector in which you operate, and your appetite for conflict. A challenger brand eats conflict for breakfast, and generally has a good story to tell as a consequence. A charity or a pharmaceutical company has a clear and urgent fight to fight, and so by identifying the conflict at the heart of its offer, it can build a core narrative that casts itself as the heroic champion of a manifest need. A little conflict goes a long way in this field. So a bank may wish to tread carefully when identifying the need it meets, to remain in the zone of credibility or comfort.

And yet every brand should be able to articulate its offer, and that offer needs to supply a need and inevitably solve its customer's problems. Problems imply conflicts, and resolution of conflicts is what stories love to get stuck into. It's best to think big and heroically in these passages dedicated to conflict, as you can always tone it down later when you come to share your tale.

The next challenge involves proving you have what it takes. This is where the big story idea symbolised by your Grail gets real, with some feet-on-the-ground examples to support it. As some of the most compelling narratives carry the legend, 'based on a true story', so one of the best ways of ensuring a corporate story can deliver on its promises is to found it on anecdotal evidence residing in the company. As I explain in more detail in my chapter dedicated to storytelling in Employee Engagement, getting people to share stories of what they value about the company can provide a powerful means of building a shared sense of belief and belonging in an organisation. And it can unearth some promising material to use in developing and supporting the core brand narrative.

Such anecdotes constitute a form of corporate wisdom; and gaining special wisdom is a key stage in most quest narratives. Such wisdom might just provide the magic keys to unlock the insights needed to complete the quest. Narrative riches might be found in the anecdotal treasure you already have.

And so, after a series of trials, setbacks, and crises, the hero gets close to fulfilling the mission. He or she then usually suffers a near-fatal reversal of fortunes towards the end, demanding one final burst of heroic resourcefulness. Do you really have what it takes to deliver what you propose? The people, products, processes, culture to make the story you tell a consistent reality? Could you tell it now, and be able to deliver on what it promises? Probably not. Or if you could, it may be your Grail is quite visionary enough, and you are missing an opportunity for using your story to move your business into a new reality. So what needs to change? Are you prepared to see this through? This involves some real soul searching, and will probably raise some doubts and dissent about going forward.

The archetypal quest narrative often involves at least one trip to the Underworld at a critical moment such as this. The hero is confronted by shades of the departed who impart vital knowledge, or issue warnings that help complete the quest. Similarly, you may need to employ your equivalent of this experience by invoking the epitaphs you devised earlier. If you turn back now, falter in your resolve, and not complete your quest, are you content to have this as the final word for your story?

# the esolution

As the journey comes to a close, we have to think about the return to reality, to the light of common day. So the resolution is where we gather all the various strands together, and tie up any loose ends. This involves rigorously selecting the ideas and anecdotes that deserve to survive the journey. How will these work in the world you inhabit? How will that world need to change to accommodate them? And so the final scenes involve one final taking stock, to be sure you are quite clear about the implications of the new world your story promises.

Again it is really useful to visualise things, to picture the new reality in all its detail. What will it look like, feel like, and sound like in the way this story is told? What will people now say about you? Are the values you set out with still useful to you? Does the wisdom you have gained demand a different outlook and image? A whole new identity? Rewrite those headlines according to the new story. If there's time you might even re-visit those epitaphs, and write new ones. We are now thinking about narrative closure, and so have to accept that every hero's story has, as well as a beginning and a middle, an end. And this is The End, my friend.

the
equel

Actually, it's not. It's only the beginning. The workshop may have ended, the show is over. But as the lights go up, and we trudge through popcorn and post-it notes back to our desks the real story begins. Not just the story you tell, but the story you now have to live…

That sentence fell a little flat even as I typed it. We all know that brands have to be 'lived' if they are to deliver on their promises. But we also know how difficult this is to put into practice. Brands are difficult things to live, because they are not in themselves alive. As a noun 'brand' is an abstraction that needs other things or other people to make it real and give it life. As a verb it acts on these things, branding them by conferring meaning through association. It is up to those things then to carry those meanings, either passively if they are the inanimate objects (physical collateral bearing the attributes of corporate identity); or actively if they are humans responsible for behaving in ways that support the claims made in the brand's name.

Although deriving from the realm of ideas and forged through the medium of words, stories are inherently about actions, behaviour, events, relationships and experiences. And it is through behaviour and experience that most corporate brands deliver on their promises, and build their relationships. So, whilst a brand is a difficult thing to be part of, story is perfect for participation, allowing people to identify their own roles and goals within the tale that it tells. A 'telling' is also a reckoning. By road-testing your brand story in this way you are preparing it for the rigours of the real journey ahead, when story becomes experience and delivers the promise of your brand. Knowing where you are going with your story can inspire people to go on the journey with you. It can therefore ultimately bring about much greater unity within an organisation, so you can present a much more coherent identity and a more consistent story to the world. Stories are often circular, and can set up a virtuous circle where narrative and reality seamlessly join. The story you tell will then reflect the story you live, and become the story others share about you.

Journeys within journeys. We're actually talking about three here, and at least three possible stories emerging from this scripting process:

1. Your journey of self-knowledge to discover and determine what your story needs to be all about

2. The narrative journey of the story you develop, serving as the surrogate for the journey and relationship you propose taking your customers on

3. That relationship itself, the journey you go on and the stories it generates as a lived reality.

We've already been on the first journey. We now need to think about the second.

# Developing your core story

So, you have your story. A quest romance full of valiant deeds, inspiring visions, and a thrilling, but thoroughly road-tested resolution. You can now share it with the world. Not quite yet. It would be great if a four-hour or even full-day workshop provided good-to-go content, ready to flow into the homepage or 'about us' pages of your corporate website, or the introduction to a brochure or annual report. What you have has great potential. But, as they say in Hollywood: 'it still needs work'. The real business of telling a story that's fit for your purposes starts now, drawing on the experience and insights afforded by going on the quest. The quest generated the raw material for your story, but not the story itself. The Once upon a time … of our narrative helped to identify the heroic 'who' of the drama we scripted. But this doesn't necessarily mean you should lead with 'Once upon a time there was a company that did X'. You have to tell your story differently. You don't simply replay the narrative scripted in the session. In fact, you reverse it.

You reverse a lot of things now. You shouldn't start by talking about the hero and his (your) world. Because when you start to tell your story, you are no longer the hero. Your audience is. It's no longer all about you; but about the world you will create for those who matter most to you, through the benefits you bring. This is ultimately what quest narratives are really all about, and what explains their enduring appeal. The hero's role is that of saviour. But he or she is only a means to an end.

The interests of heroes and superheroes are generally subordinate to the greater good of the communities they serve. The collective cause may even involve their individual sacrifice (remember Campbell included Christ as one of the Thousand Faces of his archetypal hero). The heroes who stop serving the worlds they have saved, transformed or redeemed, or who fail to be re-integrated into these communities, either die or are rejected. They become outsiders, withdrawing to the margins, or riding off into the sunset, until they are required again in the sequel. That's the ritual function of story as a social act, serving a broader purpose than individual heroics. The compulsion factor –

what makes these stories great entertainment – is identification. The audience identifies with the hero, or rather that part of him or her they want to be in their own dreams and aspirations. This essential empathetic role stories have always fulfilled.

It is the same with your own story. This has to pass the "what's in it for me?" test, making it easy for your audiences to relate to and see themselves in the world you promise to create for them. They're not really interested in you. Sorry. But in what you can give them. Like the hero, you are merely a means to an end. So, you start with that end – the end you reached and thoroughly road-tested by going on your quest. The world you promise to enrich or redeem through the Grail should be the focus of your story. And this story should not be the epic saga of your struggles and challenges. Most of the material you generated on your own journey will probably hit the cutting room floor. But that's ok. It's done its job. The understanding and belief gained through the experience will be invaluable. A core story is not about elaboration, but distillation, summing up your offer succinctly and with some urgency. You have to grab the attention before you can grip it with your full narrative, and gratify it with the lived relationship. Remember the Movie Pitch scenario? It is now time to devise one for your own story.

But think of it as the trailer for the movie (story) you have now developed. This is a useful exercise for ensuring your core story can be summed up and delivered with the right emphasis in a limited time span. The audience are thinking about themselves, and have no time for anything that doesn't grab their attention by being relevant to their world and their needs. So, pitch your story. The story you propose to tell them about the journey you will go on together. The Movie Pitch is, of course, a version of the famous 'elevator pitch', and serves the same function. The exercise of thinking in terms of dramatic narrative, applies an extra rigour to ensure it holds together as a story worth telling or hearing. This story must grab the attention sufficiently to want people to know more, and go on the real journey. You need to imagine 'That Voice' used for about 99% of trailers (whom my colleague Mike Oliver informs me was called Don LaFontaine) thundering out… What?

# Setting out your plot

The following adds a little showbiz attention-grabbing to a classic elevator pitch formula:

> *In a world where* [define the problem or need.................], *only* [your brand] *is the* [superlative + descriptor..............] *for* [your target market]. *This is because only your brand* [has these special qualities setting it apart] *which means that* [it benefits your key market]. *And* [perhaps saves the world].

Ok, maybe the last part is getting a bit carried away, but your vision might slot in there if it is inspiring enough. And I'm not suggesting you have to adopt Mr LaFontaine's voice when you come to pitch your story (especially if you actually are in an elevator when the opportunity arises). This exercise provides one further rigorous test for your story. If you can define the benefit; the problem you solve; why it is different and makes a difference; why people should care; and why you are best placed to deliver it, you have everything you need to start telling your story, and elaborating on how you can fulfil these promises. As Mike Oliver puts it, "we need to be as singular as the great Don Lafontaine himself, who actually wrote the words he intoned, in summing up our context and offer as clearly and concisely as possible".

The trailer leads to the movie; the movie is then experienced; this experience then lives in the imagination through identification. It becomes the audience's story. You are seeking to establish a similar chain. The Movie Pitch discipline provides the wherewithal to set it in motion, ensuring the elements are in place, by relying on the time honoured means Hollywood has perfected to grab the attention, before it grips and gratifies with the product itself.

## *Telling your core story*

The Movie Pitch is but the tip of your story's iceberg. It provides the succinct expression of your brand story, but rests on the strong foundations of knowledge, proven substance and real-life anecdote gained on your quest. As such, a core story is very much like a brand positioning, road-tested for narrative application. Putting it through the rigours of narrative gives it a coherent plot, ensuring it has everything in place for sharing it with the world. Because it is already narrative, it closes the gap between ideas and their expression, and makes the passage from abstraction to action more fluid and achievable. Brand developed as story brings us one step closer to sharing this consistently across communications, and delivering it as an experience. That, for me, is the main contribution that story can bring to business and branding, providing a rigorous but richly rewarding vehicle for carrying out communications needs.

Yet, I don't want to suggest there is a one-size-fits-all formula to corporate storytelling. Story brings discipline and a rigour, but it shouldn't be a straightjacket.

A core story should provide the cloth from which you cut the coat of your specific communications needs. Different channels and applications demand different ways of telling the core story, tailored to specific circumstances. Story, at its most basic, is the right words in the right order to achieve the right effect on the right people. That order, and the emphasis it brings, is likely to change in response to those circumstances.

Take the Movie Pitch exercise for distilling the core story into a succinct form. This is a variation of what I call the Wow, How, Who narrative structure. I mentioned this earlier when I explained how we used this to help a technology company cut to the chase of a complex offer on its corporate website. We actually essayed this story first for a PowerPoint presentation, designed to generate interest among potential investment partners. In both cases, there was a need to grab the attention of non-specialists with a clear and compelling articulation of the benefits, before going on to explain how this might be accomplished and why these are the only people who can do it.

Wow, How, Who is perfect for occasions and applications such as these, when you cannot guarantee any prior knowledge of the company; any detailed or technical grasp of the subject; or much time or attention span. If you don't grab the attention on the homepage, or in the small window of opportunity you have to convince very rich, seen-it-all-before people why they should give you their attention (let alone their millions), you have lost your chance to explain the How or the Who. All that is now immaterial. The show has moved on. Yet so many companies are caught up in What they do and Who they are, they lose the focus on Why this matters, and neglect to make clear first and foremost Why anyone should care. Lose this focus, and you have already lost the audience. These companies may have a great story to tell, but they tell it in the wrong order for the specific audience or opportunity.

It's sometimes useful to think of your story in terms of a pyramid, then decide what needs to go at the apex. It wouldn't be a business book without a few models, but I think this is a useful and a very simple one for thinking about narrative structure when sharing a core story. It can help to ensure the right messages are in the right order for the right audience and channel. Why a pyramid? Because pyramids have structural integrity built into them, helping to visibly reinforce the core principle of narrative coherence. They have geometrical and mathematical associations, which are apt for expressing the logical rigour of good storytelling. Yet their association with one of the oldest civilisations, who told hieroglyphic stories on these edifices we don't yet fully understand, also gives them an ancient authority and imaginative allure. They were made for telling stories, and have generated countless stories in turn. Besides, the basic triangular structure is perfect for emphasising the need to have a succinct, sharply-focused message uppermost in your story, resting on all the thinking and messages that supports this top-line message and ensures it all stands up.

*Wow* – the benefit-led offer succinctly summed up

*How* – What you uniquely have to deliver this offer

*Who* – why you are the people to deliver this, and why we should believe you

Many companies tend to have an inverted pyramid as the structure for their story. They often try to provide all the details about what they do and who they are up front. And so the story falls over. The more detail you have to impart, the more complicated the messages, the further down the pyramid these should be. If you attempt to cram them all into the apex of your story pyramid, it's all pulled out of shape, grows top heavy, becomes inverted and topples over. Thinking in terms of a story pyramid for a website is perfect. You only have a very small window to grab attention, so you need enough Wow there at the outset, to ensure the relationship deepens as the story journey develops. (Those who are familiar with the inverted pyramid model proposed by journalism and PR might be puzzled by what I suggest, but it's not so very different, despite my inverted emphasis. Yes, you should put everything that's important at the top, but this should be succinctly expressed to provide a discipline to ensure it is clear and singular in its focus. By being succinctly compelling you encourage readers to stay for the How and the Who, which can be elaborated in more detail below.)

That's not to say there isn't a place for what might be termed 'eloquent details'. These are used very powerfully in fiction, and find their counterpart, if used judiciously, in corporate communications. The eloquent detail of a man's footprint provides the main turning point in Daniel Defoe's *Robinson Crusoe*, informing the lonely castaway that he has human company on his island. And of course details in the form of clues are essential to detective, spy and mystery narratives. Similarly, a choice example (maybe an innovative product or groundbreaking material as the star of a short piece of video) might speak volumes about your approach and what makes you special, far more effectively than reams of adjectives attempting to say what you could more eloquently show. You will know your business, and if you start to find your voice and understand your unique story, you will instinctively know where these riches reside.

Nor is it to say that Wow should be uppermost every time. You will know what's right for your story, and thinking in terms of a pyramid helps to determine the ordering of core messages and appropriate use of detail. Who (you) might actually be what gives your story its Wow, and in some circumstances this may be the message you need to lead with. Who, is of course, an important component in any story. A story needs a hero. And whilst that might ultimately be the customer or another important stakeholder, people buy from people. Emotional connection is vital to storytelling, and there is a time and a place to bring this to the fore.

Indeed, as Annette Simmons argues, it is always essential to establish Who it is telling the story upfront. Her excellent book *The Story Factor* delves deep into the psychology of story, and the many ways it can be used to win people over. Even those predisposed not to believe or trust in you. As she argues, people have often formed their own stories about you, before you attempt to utter a word. Telling a personal story at the offset, or a parable that illustrates a different view point, is likely to change their views, and put them in a more receptive frame of mind to hear what you have to say. And whilst Simmons is mostly concerned with how the persuasive power of story works in 'live' situations, such as presentations or meetings, her insights and suggestions are useful for thinking about the more indirect or virtual encounters many communications entail.

You can't control the stories others might already be telling about you, based on scant evidence, hearsay, or simply the endemic mistrust attending the dog-eat-dog world of business. These might be stories such as "I can't afford your services", or "You're too big/small for my needs", or simply "I've heard it all before". These are emotional barriers, based on half-formed, often unconscious, sentiments rather than concrete facts. As such, countering these barriers with a whole lot of rational evidence is unlikely to get you very far. You can only fight story with story. It is there to build bridges, and make connections. As Simmons puts it: "A story is more respectful than telling someone what he or she ought to think. Respect connects. Once you have connected, you are ready to move your listener, step-by-step, to see the world as you see it". And whilst no one-size-fits-all for story, understanding its dynamics and applying its principles will enable your own story to eventually triumph in the only place it is likely to have any real influence: the emotional and imaginative sphere.

I instinctively felt the need for this when I started to write the book you are now holding. And so my own story pyramid starts with Who uppermost. You don't know me from Adam, and so I have to establish some credible authority for addressing you on this subject. My own story tells of my professional experience in both literary and commercial contexts. I can hope this experience goes some way to authenticating the views I want to share with you, and establishes a measure of authority in seeking to do this. You need to know who I am before you are prepared to even consider what I have to say. If you are in a bookshop or browsing a retail site, you are potentially in the market to be told or sold a story. Whilst the cover blurb should seek to entice you with a bit of Wow, pretty soon I have to back this up with the Who, before going into the Why, What, How and Where of storytelling. Wow, How, Who is great for when there is no time and no necessary inclination to be told a story. But you are not always in this situation, so you need to be flexible with your approach.

Sometimes, as Simmons, suggests, you need to take it slow, or you will scare the horses. Rush in with the facts, rational arguments or hard sell, and people immediately switch off. Tell people a story, and you might slowly win them round. And whilst I have argued that stories need to have clarity, Simmons suggests that part of their persuasive power can be in ambiguity or unfinished nature, allowing people enough room to form their own conclusions or morals from the tale they are told.

Stories should not deliver dogma, and their greatest appeal is to the imagination. Or, as Andrew Staton, a professional screenwriter put it in a recent TED lecture: "don't give your audience 4, give them 2 + 2". The brain loves to solve problems, and be involved in completing things. Stories allow it to do this. A story really starts to live in the imagination when it is completed by the recipient; turning the 2 + 2 into 4 on the intellectual level, and identifying with the core emotional truths it holds by applying them to our own lives and stories. It achieves this most effectively by not being so rigidly defined.

There's such a thing as being too direct. Storytelling, as the masters of the craft know well, is often the art of seduction. I once saw a strapline for a bank which boldly declared "We want your business". "You don't say", I thought (actually something ruder). But it set me wondering about why this was such a lousy strapline, despite having the best intentions. You can see what it's trying to do, dispense with tricksy word play or airy promises, by making an honest appeal to the consumer as straight-talking adults. But it both says too much, and not enough. By blurting out what is effectively the basic premise of all marketing, nay, all commercial transactions, it fails to even begin to tell a story. You want my business? So do they, and them, and them. And who cares what you want anyway? What about what I want? As my mother always used to tell me, "I want doesn't get". Try a bit harder. Tell me a story.

It occurred to me that the addition of a single word 'because' at least starts to tell a story. Now I'm a bit more intrigued, and prepared to imagine all the things this bank might be prepared to show me to prove this point. "Because we want your business" still isn't the greatest strapline in the world. But it at least implies a benefit to me and starts to take me on a journey. It starts *In media res* (in the middle of things, where so many great stories start). It could either be the sign-off to a compelling testament proving why the bank wants my business, or the start of that conversation. It has implied back story (the unspoken proofs to a question I don't remember asking) and forward momentum, the incitement to discover Why and How. The addition of one word says so much more, by not attempting to say everything. Give them 2 + 2, not 4.

And so, in the spirit of indeterminacy, I should observe that the principles explained in the first half of this book should not be treated as cast-iron rules or inflexible formulas. The whole point of using story in this context is to cut through the cliché and codswallop with something that communicates authentically by connecting emotionally. The last thing I want to do is to turn an intuitive and human impulse into a mechanistic dogma or set of tricks. These are principles, not rules, to be observed but also adapted when occasion demands. Because they are based on intuitive and time-honoured practices that work within the grain or our brains, understanding them and applying them with confidence will in time make telling your story *as a story* second nature.

It's now time to consider how all this might be applied in appropriate ways to the day-to-day business of corporate communications.

chapter four
# Where to Tell your Story

——

Where to tell your story? I suppose the short and predictable answer is "just about everywhere". Every communication you issue, every experience you provide, should express the same story, and serve all your audiences. It's no mystery why companies often fail to do this. Inconsistency on the outside so often reflects a similar fragmentation internally. Organisational silos inevitably lead to inconsistent storytelling. So we often find the makings of a really good story on a company's Sustainability pages or report, but nothing like the focus, authenticity or imagination on its homepage, 'About us', or Annual Report. Or we might find a recruitment ad or microsite – because they derive from something called *Human* Resources – reflecting a more approachable side, but scant evidence of this elsewhere. This is a problem.

So many companies appear to be suffering from an identity crisis when it comes to telling their story. Whilst narrative inconsistency is unlikely to be a conscious policy, it can be deeply problematic when seeking to inspire trust. Different stories for different audiences suggests a company is speaking with a forked tongue. If your story fragments, your identity fragments. If you lose the plot you lose your audiences, or at least a measure of their trust. A customer or stakeholder relationship is a journey. If the thread breaks, so does the relationship. Story demands a thread, but it also provides one: connecting across as well as within the stories you tell. The plot of your story – the space you mark out, and the strategic focus and direction this allows – therefore must be connected across, as much as coherently expressed within, all communications and experiences. That is where true 'integrity' lies, and with it, credibility and trust built.

That does not mean your story shouldn't be adaptable to specific needs, contexts and channels. Which is what this part of the book is all about. The following short chapters take us on a rather selective tour through the communications landscape, involving disciplines or channels with which I have direct experience. In each I briefly consider the role of storytelling in these particular areas, briefly touching on what could probably sustain whole books in their own rights.

So. Where to start? Whilst we still have the smell of popcorn in our nostrils, and the movie theme ringing in our ears, it makes sense to stay in the world of showbiz. The first examples of where to tell a story are applications where the narrative and dramatic arts are (or should be) intuitively applied. In one case they are often over-applied, and the other woefully neglected. We'll start with Film and PowerPoint, the most showbizzy applications in the armoury of corporate storytelling practice.

# Through Film

—

This is an area where story naturally belongs, providing an opportunity to unleash the inner director, revved up but ultimately restrained in our hypothetical story-development workshop. With film, storytelling is no longer *like* Hollywood, a set of principles to apply: it *is* Hollywood. And so the narrative essayed in the session, scaled down and succinctly expressed in your 'trailer', can now be given Technicolor, Dolby Stereo, Panoramic, Epic exposure in a homepage or boardroom near you. Right?

Wrong. I did say storytelling in practice might involve a bit of rule bending or breaking. Here, straightaway, is a prime example of this. Film is ironically the last place needing to look to Hollywood for inspiration when it comes to telling a corporate story. In fact, it should look away, applying other lessons from the principles of storytelling that lead it gently from the grand epic highways to more humble routes to the same end: moving human beings.

I'm not suggesting you should junk all the principles I've so earnestly proffered as a theory, now we finally come to apply them in practice. Especially not here. Film is what could be called a natural or even 'pure' storytelling medium. And so it pre-eminently demands clarity of theme, coherence of thread, and especially emotional connection. That's why it is such a useful model for thinking about a core brand story. It would be a shocking waste of the medium if we then failed to use it for what the moving image does best: moving people through the power of storytelling. And we, who have grown up with countless examples of professional cinematic storytelling before us, have high expectations of what is possible through the medium. And that, paradoxically, is where the problem lies. Because we have such iconic examples before us, there is a strong temptation to emulate the tricks and trappings of the greats when we come to tell a corporate story through film. And so doing, radically and disastrously misapply the power of narrative to serve different objectives.

The Hollywood movie is a finely-tuned instrument for moving people for entertainment ends. It applies all the principles I have identified to grip people and gratify them through emotional connection and identification. Need to heighten that emotion? No problem, here's some soaring sentimental music to underscore the effect represented by the actors, and ensure there isn't a dry eye left in the house. It does all these things because that is its job. Corporate communications have a different job. And whilst they should be emotionally engaging, even entertaining, these things are a means to an end, and not an end in themselves. Cinematic storytelling is strong stuff. Narrative and emotive dynamite, to be handled with extreme care in the corporate communications context.

The problem is, it isn't on the whole. Too many corporate videos emulate Hollywood but end up looking amateur. We have also grown up with the best examples of pop or classical music before us, but we wouldn't dream of booking a stadium or standing in front of an audience to perform our debut on electric guitar or grand piano. So why think we are the next Steven Spielberg just because someone hands us a movie camera, an edit suite and a modest budget?

This may sound rather harsh, but it's extraordinary how many companies use video to lavishly achieve little. The same soaring music that tugs at the heartstrings in a stirring epic of heroic endeavour or romantic comedy, ends up being simply cheesy when it accompanies scenes of manufacturing, corporate edifices or the stellar trajectory of a share price. Emotional connection shouldn't be achieved with a cattle prod, compelling the audience to feel something the content itself cannot muster. It may stir the audience momentarily (if it doesn't have them gagging or squirming), but it ends up imparting no message, and is therefore a wasted opportunity of a highly effective storytelling medium.

There are wasted opportunities every where you look. Video, by definition, is a visual medium, and so showing is far more effective than saying here. And yet so many corporate videos rely on written captions to tell their stories (the age of silent movies being well and truly past). Or talking heads, delivering monotonous monologues in dull generic settings. The fact that they often also supply a transcript of the address suggests an instinctive awareness of where this content really belongs. Videos are often used to convey information, which isn't where their greatest strengths lie. They merely inform, when they should really seek to inspire.

Or when they seek to inspire, they go so far towards the other extreme they end up conveying very little you can usefully take away from the experience. Here we find companies attempting to say and show everything on a vast scale, yet without the narrative or selective focus effective storytelling demands. Too many corporate videos are effectively animated lists of everything the company does and where it does it, montaged together with suitably bombastic music to match the epic scale or the panoramic vistas of global dominance the company depicts.

## *Show real*

I've said corporate stories always need to get real, to show how what the company does touches people in the real world, and why this ultimately matters. They need to do it here too. In fact, it's what the medium does best. The moving image is made for moving people with stories about people. And yet too often this opportunity is squandered, ending up with what Dean Beswick, Head of Moving Image at Radley Yeldar, terms 'corporate wallpaper'. His insights encouraged my demolition of the worst excesses of this medium. But what does he suggest companies should be doing instead?

For a start they need to scale things down. Don't always try to tell the Big Story. You don't have the budget, the screen ratio or the timeframe to compete with the Hollywood epic drama. And you're not there to entertain. Dean therefore suggests documentaries are a far more useful genre for getting a company's story across. They don't try to say everything; but focus on real issues that matter to people. This keeps things to a human scale and make the benefits and messages tangible. Stories work best when your audience can identify with the issues or individuals depicted. And they can't do that if you try to show everything you do, or talk about it in abstract or grandiose terms.

Even Hollywood doesn't always adopt the high epic mode when telling its Biggest Stories. Its heroes are not always superheroes, but often just ordinary Joes we can identify with, caught up in momentous events. War films usually aren't about wars anymore, and rarely about the generals. The world events provide the backdrop for human-scale universal dramas. War gives the story context (why the individuals face the challenges they do), humanity gives it relevance and emotional resonance. Similarly the big issues or challenges a company tackles are more credibly evoked if particularised and humanised on a smaller scale. As Dean puts it: "By focusing on the right detail, paradoxically you can tell a broader corporate story. So instead of trying to say everything, just say one important thing that's meaningful, tangible, and above all engaging". The particular becomes the universal, and the personal gives your corporate brand personality. This is the literary principle known as 'synecdoche', where a single part stands for the whole idea, and it can work very powerfully in a short film where an eloquent detail can speak volumes about a company.

I once saw a series of films about innovative materials, where those responsible for the inventions explained why they were so pioneering, and the use to which they would be put. These short narratives were, by definition, highly detailed; but were far more convincing and eloquent of the company's 'innovation', than any claims they could make with talking heads or soaring music. What's more, the genuine enthusiasm the inventors had for their creations was infectious, and made the emotional connection (despite the highly technical subject), far more effectively than any aesthetic embellishments.

# Sound and vision

Telling stories with sight and sound gives your brand life, and can capture the 'tone of voice' of your brand far more effectively than any guidelines attempting to describe this in words. As I've repeatedly said, emotional connection is essential if a story is going to really communicate something. And emotion is what film does better than any other medium in the communications toolkit. Film can explore a whole range of emotions that simply cannot be conveyed in written text. It has a licence to be emotional, and through this licence connects with people who allow themselves to be moved. Humour can be genuinely funny, where in bare text it might fall flat; tragedy can underline the importance of an issue by bringing it into the realm of lived reality and make an individual story represent a universal need.

We know this. It's why we go to the cinema. And it's why, despite all the technological breakthroughs that supposedly defy distance, we still prefer to meet people face-to-face and attend important meetings in person. People connect with people. We're wired to do it, and video is the most powerful surrogate for such real-time connections. Done well, film can show the human impact of your story, and the human face of your business, by people embodying it. Real people, that is. Don't just let the CEO or Director of Something Important tell your story – they will do that at the AGM or in the pages of the FT – but extend the cast list to allow those close to those eloquent details to show why these make your story vital and interesting. Replace talking heads with acting people. Not acting in the scripted (insincere) sense, but the opposite. Real people in real situations displaying genuine emotion about why what they do matters.

User-Generated Video (UGV) is a very useful tool in this respect, and has become a familiar aspect of the social media landscape through the likes of YouTube. For a start it's cost-efficient. Budget might not allow you to send a film crew to Kuala Lumpa, but you can send a flip camera with instructions and guidelines to employees around the globe and gather some great content. And whilst these guidelines are important for getting the best results, the 'hand held' rawness or naivety of the results are more easy to forgive than the failed Hollywood pretensions of many corporate efforts.

But the main benefit is the life it brings to illustrate and substantiate your story. Instead of talking about 'innovation', 'service' or the 'values that set you apart', let the people who embody or deliver these things bring them to life. Why talk about 'solutions' in abstract terms, when you can allow someone who solved a massive problem for you or a customer show it at work. By telling smaller, real stories, your bigger story is told far more credibly and compellingly. A series of short documentaries or mini-diaries dedicated to specific issues opens a clear window on your business and its culture.

## *Show business*

Sometimes there is a need to get information across, and the right film genre can do this far more effectively than print or presentations. Animation often is perfect for this. If you have something complicated or new to get across an animated film can turn this into an engaging and easy-to-digest story. As Dean puts it, "animation is to diagrams and illustrations, what video is to photographs". Motion makes it eye-catching and involving, and allows you to tell a story that turns raw information into a digestible coherent narrative. It can 'dramatise data', two words you don't often see coupled together, but possible in this medium. If Information can be 'beautiful', when presented in elegant infographics, you can add the extra kinetic dimension by setting that beauty in motion.

You can illustrate scale, history, and the relationship between things far more succinctly than attempting to explain this, and so can tell a complex story simply. You can *animate* concepts, showing how elements come together, and thus make them live and have reality in the imaginations of your audiences. This can scale things down to pure iconic information which allows you to convey big ideas in tangible digestible forms. Animation allows you to use visual metaphors that can convey complex ideas in immediately recognisable, engaging and memorable ways. Metaphor means 'to carry over', with meaning being carried over by something else. In a dynamic medium such as film, it can carry ideas even further and more effectively, carrying audiences with you by involving them in the story your metaphors convey.

There's also something about animation that takes us right back to our earliest days as story consumers. If you're like me, you probably spent much of your formative years glued to the 'goggle box', where programmes designed for children were generally animated. I believe they still are. As these usually had an educative dimension, I suspect we unconsciously associate the genre with the pleasures of learning. Whilst all stories tend to put us in a more receptive frame of mind for learning things, animation may have a special place in our individual memories as the ultimate – because primary – narrative genre. Deeper still perhaps, if you imagine the effect of a cave painting flickering in torchlight. Animation perhaps connects atavistically, with a uniquely deep power to impart essential information.

But doesn't animation lack that human touch I've been banging on about? Dean insists you can still achieve this powerfully through characterisation and voice. People relate to animated characters on very intimate terms. "Does Jessica Rabbit lack the human touch"? Good point. Animated characters don't get stage fright. And if you want to be representative of geography, gender or nationality, this can save you a fortune.

Animation is also great for bringing brand (corporate identity) elements into a story. The film can be branded through and through with colourways and other graphic assets you might own. These elements can help provide a visual continuity that ensures your story threads together aesthetically as well as conceptually. Because it is not confined by space, time or any physical constraints imposed on human actors and locations, the sky's the limit on what you can employ to tell your story. It can provide a richly rewarding expression of your brand by appealing on multi-sensual levels to ensure it really connects. If you can think it, you can dramatise it with animation.

So, maybe you really can be the Spielberg of corporate comms after all.

# Through PowerPoint

Few tools in the corporate communications box are so often used and abused (in all senses) as this one. We all complain about 'death by PowerPoint', have probably experienced it at point blank range, and have sworn never to put others through the ordeal ourselves. Yet boardroom massacres are still a sad reality of modern corporate life. Everyday countless victims are found slumped in their chairs, their brains bored hollow with bullet points, their dying wish that the presenter had just told them a story. The medium, like those victims, is crying out for it. If corporate video tends to encourage too much misapplied showbiz, PowerPoint suffers from a pronounced deficit of what would turn an ordeal into an experience. This is one area that could benefit from applying the narrative and dramatic arts much more directly.

A PowerPoint presentation is after all a show. It is a live performance, with a captive audience. You can look them in the eyes, and create the emotional rapport upon which trust is built. It provides the perfect opportunity to employ some narrative and dramatic magic to have them eating out of your hands. The spotlight is on you, the audience are hushed and expectant... And that, alas, is the problem.

Anticipated stage fright often takes over, encouraging presenters to focus more on the content of their individual slides than the overall performance. In so doing they not only squander a perfect opportunity to engage people with a story, they misapply the whole purpose of the medium. The result? Something that would be better served up as a document to be read (or not). I know it's easy to knock PowerPoint, and we all know we could do it a whole lot better. Be better rehearsed, more confident, rely on notes less, make eye contact more. Yet, somehow our resolve crumbles the next time we need to put a presentation together under pressure. "I'd rather get my content right, before worrying about the show itself", we claim. And before we know it we have those towering walls of content no one can scale; lists without narrative thread, and a dead document we then attempt to resuscitate through amateur animations.

I'm not talking about presentation skills here. I'm no expert on that, I know there are plenty out there, and could do with their help myself. I'm simply talking about building a bit more narrative art into the PowerPoint experience. Thus turning a necessary evil into a more effective storytelling vehicle. If the showbiz magic of presentation skills represents the ultimate ideal; and the usual, too much content, crammed into a literary document turned live ordeal, is our starting point, we can at least aim for a middle ground. Pushing the dial more towards the 'performance' end whilst remaining in the comfort zone of "I need to get the content right". Getting the content right is really all I'm talking about here. The right content in the right order to achieve the right effect on the audience. Story, at its most basic. It's all about content and control. Remaining in control of the material, and of the audience for which it is designed, by using the medium for what it was designed: connecting with and convincing those audiences.

Which first of all means reversing the emphasis of that content and its role. Presenters who use slide content as a thread to get *them* through are unlikely to be telling a compelling story, because they've stopped thinking about their audience. We all do it. It's less terrifying to stand up there if we at least know our slides have everything we need, and we can talk from them. In other words, prompt notes publically displayed – the rope we throw across the chasm of our presentation, saving us from improvisation freefall. But by thinking about our own needs we neglect those of the limp, lifeless victims we lose along the way. The thread shouldn't be there to reassure us we know what comes next, but to make our audience, like any successfully gripped by story, wonder 'what happens next?'

Wilkie Collins, friend of Dickens, and highly popular author of sensational fictions in his own right, summed up the storyteller's art in the dictum: "Make 'em laugh. Make 'em cry. Make 'em wait". Whilst it would be unwise to string it out as long as Collins's own serial monsters (amounting to over a thousand pages at times), it wouldn't hurt to bring some of this artistry into the humble PowerPoint presentation. After all, the audience is captive, you have their attention. It's yours to lose. And with it, no doubt, a lot more besides.

PowerPoint therefore involves a different dynamic from the homepage or a piece of direct mail, where you have about a nanosecond to grab attention before they click or fling away. A different setting allows you to use a different story pyramid, which really does take them on a journey. You don't need to blow all your 'Wow' up front. Save some for the finale, learning from the masters of the art. You wouldn't give the punch line or reveal whodunit in the first sentence, so, when you have a captive audience and a dramatic narrative medium, use it to full effect. Surprise them. According to movie man Peter Guber, surprise is an essential in storytelling. *"Expectation + violation of expectation"* is what every successful storyline needs to deliver. And what better place to deploy this principle, than a setting where the expectations are not particularly high. Defying expectations will make them sit up and listen, allowing you to deliver your story to a captivated as well as captive audience.

Defy expectations, but do so on sure narrative foundations. PowerPoint is effectively a dramatic medium, so the rules of the well-made drama apply. When I first mentioned Aristotle's dramatic principles, I made clear I wasn't suggesting you model your own story on a Greek Tragedy. A happy ending, after all, is the outcome both you and your audiences are probably seeking. Yet, there is a lot to be learned from Aristotle's outline for a three-act drama that can be applied directly and usefully to some PowerPoint presentations. A credentials presentation is a perfect example. This suggestion comes from a communications trainer called Greg Keen, and is really useful here. Keen urges companies to use the Aristotelian three-act tragic structure when presenting to potential customers or partners. And, as the essence of drama is conflict, he encourages companies to be quite honest about the struggles they've been through, the challenges they've faced, and even the mistakes they've made.

I know it sounds counterintuitive to dwell on your mistakes when the objective is to convince potential partners or customers of your competence, but that's kind of the point. It defies expectations but it also makes a whole lot of sense. It takes some nerve, but then it displays some too. The reward is getting the audience on your side through the involving arts of storytelling. If you admit to struggles and explain how you have overcome them, you demonstrate resourcefulness and a determination to succeed (heroic stuff). And if you can show what you have learned (how you have grown) by what happened, you can deliver a moral to the story which is likely to resonate powerfully with your audience.

The example Keen demonstrates is a hypothetical company's losing its way, going back to basics and listening to what its customers really want. Remember, every hero has his or her flaws. It's what makes them human, and encourages us to identify with them, and find out how they respond to the challenges the narrative throws at them. The same dramatic/psychological principle operates here. The humility creates sympathy; the narrative encourages empathy; and the learning it demonstrates suggests a direct benefit to the potential client. So much more powerful and convincing than saying "we always listen to our customers". Anyone can say that, and they usually do. But if you can explain why anecdotally you are more likely to be believed. Mistakes are human. Humans buy from humans, and they also love hearing their stories.

The abilities to respond to challenges and solve problems also sends a powerful message if dramatised in this way. After all, if you're pitching your services or solutions, your audience more than likely face a few challenges themselves. What business doesn't? By showing your mettle in this way you are demonstrating that you are a reliable 'ally' to the real hero of the story. Them. Nearly every hero has an ally (as Keen points out), and this is a great way of establishing rapport through narrative. You get to introduce yourself – essential if they don't know that much about you, and for creating the human connection that will get them on your side – but you don't go on about yourself. It's all about them, drawing them into your story as the masters of the craft have always done, by allowing us to recognise ourselves in the mirrors they hold up to us. You involve them in your story, imaginatively at first; but then, all being well, in reality through the business you do together. The same satisfaction the brain achieves from solving problems is gained by seeing them solved in narrative. Stories – dramatic stories showing conflicts overcome – are, problem-solving vehicles.

Potential tragedy, averted into triumph can thus turn the usual plod through a company's credentials into a compelling, surprising but convincing journey. "We always listen to customers" is simply a statement. "And that's why we always listen to customers", as the payoff of a plausible illustrative anecdote, involves them in your story, and gets them on your side.

There is often the 'killer' question at pitch presentations, putting the presenter on the back foot by asking him or her about their biggest challenge, or to confess to an occasion when things went horribly wrong in a professional relationship. This is usually to catch the presenter out, and thrown at him or her in the spirit of conflict. How much better to have used the homeopathic principle of admitting to mistakes or near catastrophes up front, rather than having to defend what you've left out of your sanitised version. A good response simply shows your resourcefulness under pressure. Triumphing over adversity shows you have what it takes to win, long term. And, if nothing else, your narrative is more likely to keep them awake, to find out what happened. So, when you do get to deliver your account of the triumph and what it taught you, you have their full attention, you have won their admiration, and possibly more. This may even be the beginning of a beautiful relationship.

Now that's a story ending everybody loves.

# Through Annual Reporting

After all this showbiz and drama, it's maybe time to come down to earth. With a bump, by immersing ourselves in the sober world of investor relations. Presided over by accountants and company secretaries, and adhering to its own conventions, protocols and language, Annual Reporting is an area particularly resistant to the idea or arts of storytelling. If business really is a separate planet ruled by reason, and built on facts, then this is its very epicentre.

In some ways this is understandable, given the legislative pressures that continue to shape annual reports, with new demands appearing every year stipulating what listed companies must disclose. This is of course a response to the breakdown of trust in the corporate and financial worlds following the high-profile accounting scandals of recent history, and the retrenchment of market confidence in general. The logic behind the legislation is clear: more disclosures lead to greater transparency, and greater transparency will lead to greater accountability, which will in turn restore trust, and with it confidence. If investors can see everything, and have all the facts at their disposal about a company, they will be able to make more informed decisions, and the markets will in future be built on surer foundations. This all makes perfect rational sense. That's just how things should work if the world obeyed the laws we create for it; if people acted in wholly rational ways; and, critically, if the vehicles that have to carry these legislation-shaped disclosures didn't also have another important job to do: communicate with human beings.

Yet everything about this logical formula appears designed to inhibit effective communication, best achieved through story. With predictable results. Successive demands have generated diverse types of content by diverse hands with no clear thread, or little sense of what it all 'adds up' to. The proliferation of boxes to tick has meant the burgeoning of content, with reports expanding threefold over the last fifteen years. More disclosure doesn't necessarily mean greater transparency, if there's so much detail it's difficult to see the wood for the trees. And finally, the compelled disclosure of facts and figures itself establishes a legalistic mindset fundamentality at odds with the emotional connection story demands and trust thrives on.

Fixed protocols mould corporate stories into generic shapes, encouraging everyone to say the same things and sound the same way. The more disclosure = more trust formula is therefore potentially a self-defeating exercise when translated into a communications vehicle. This might allow analysts to compare like with like. But such reports encourage nobody to actually *like* what they read or the company behind it. In short, 'disclosure' discourages story. The very term speaks volumes. It implies that the default setting is 'closed', and the lid is reluctantly lifted each year only so wide as compliance demands. The direct antithesis of the expansive open engagement at the beating heart of storytelling.

Yet hope may well be on the horizon. For whilst so much legislation has pulled reporting in a direction unconducive to storytelling, there is growing recognition of the need for measures that would reverse this trend, or at least mitigate the tendencies box-ticking and list-making encourages. The main developments that might eventually nurture narrative can be summed up as follows:

**Cut the clutter.** Leviathan reports defeat the purpose of pro-transparency measures if the salient details are obscured by immaterial material. Reports need to be clearer in their focus and their purpose, and provide a more visible narrative thread for readers.

**Integrate.** Whilst this is principally a call for a more holistic approach to aligning financial with non-financial information, this suggests a recognition of a need to join things up, providing greater narrative coherence where there is currently fragmentation.

**Explain the business model.** It is now law in the UK for companies to include a clear explanation in their reports of how they generate value. Not just how much, but how come. Not just a relationship between a company and its shareholders, but the relationship it has with the wider world as part of a value chain that ultimately impacts on that world. Not simply an account of how it adds up (financially), but what it ultimately adds up to.

Clarity, tick. Coherence, tick. And a compelling case for why what a company does matters in the real world of people and things, tick. The new demands potentially add up to a checklist of effective storytelling. Historically pulled in one direction by compliance legislation, Annual Reporting may well be encouraged to adopt a very different path, ultimately becoming a more effective storytelling medium. As the Accounting Standards Board report 'Rising to the Challenge' put it in 2009: "Business models cannot be conveyed through numbers alone, and it is up to the narrative report to tell the story of what the company does to generate cash".

# The (Re)turn of narrative accounting

I can't help thinking the need for these developments is staggeringly obvious. Annual Reporting and the broader discipline of Investor Relations, seem tailor-made for story. It appears to be an intrinsically narrative medium, that was hijacked and hoodwinked by legislators and list-makers, but is now reclaiming its birthright.

This reminds me that the word 'account' doesn't have an exclusively financial meaning, and how in Romance languages the family resemblance between bank-telling and storytelling is more apparent. For example, in Spain the verb "contar" means both to count (numbers) and recount (a story). When you ask for your bill in a restaurant: "la cuenta" is literally a numerical account of the meal you have just enjoyed. But you also hear people saying "cuentame", meaning recount what happened, explain it, tell me the story. The word derives from Latin, and of course survives in our own words 'account' and 'count'. Una cuenta is an account (financial); un cuento is a tale or short story.

Accountants create accounts with numbers, authors with words. Language often reveals the deeper psychological connections culture and custom seek to obscure. It's as though Financial Account (involving facts, details, bottom line, analytics, and reason), was separated from its twin brother Narrative Account (fond of imagination, drama, storyline, anecdote and emotion), and they now reside in very different dominions. And whilst legislation and convention have conspired to keep them apart, there are developments that may very well bring about their reunion in due course. The reconciliation of these two estranged twins is the storyline I'd like to develop in this chapter.

Everything about Annual Reporting, in principle, points to applying a more story-focused approach. The very genre encourages a degree of retrospection unusual for corporate communications, where the moment is always Now, and the focus is invariably on the future. Reports, on the other hand, are compelled to tell stories with narrative closure. To have beginnings, middles and ends. Year ends: making sense of the year as a completed, coherent whole. Most stories involve a degree of retrospection. The word 'story' derives from 'history (again, in Romance languages they are the same word), and they are generally written from a perspective of retrospective knowledge. There is therefore everything to encourage the creator of the yearly story to give it a shape; to go beyond simply filing an account, into sharing an account. One that explains the bottom line by means of a storyline, and ultimately allows people to understand what all that financial adding up actually adds up to.

Yet, whilst the annual rhythm encourages retrospection, and imposes narrative closure, the ongoing business of Investor Relations involves a future focus and a continuous open narrative. The purpose of the report is not really looking back, but moving forward. It is there to show how this year's chapter, or better still, episode, is part of a continuing never-ending story of value-creation, driven by a clear strategic focus and a commitment to perform. Its role is ultimately to inspire confidence in a continued investment relationship. If Reporting is intrinsically a narrative genre, then the broader objective it should fulfil demands a different model to the cinematic one that has served us well up to now. If not cinema, then what?

For my money, soap opera provides the perfect analogy and narrative model.

# *Corporation Street*

There is actually much to encourage this rather surprising analogy, and much that Investor Relations can learn from one of the most successful storytelling genres. Soap opera is also defined by its open-ended, but episodic narrative. There is no end to the overall storyline, which keeps going for as long as ratings or advertising revenues hold up. This can mean over fifty years of dramatic cycles involving the same group of people in a close-knit community. Community provides continuity of values and personnel, whilst the development of multiple storylines depicting different dramas creates narrative momentum and maintains interest down the years.

These individual storylines have beginnings, middles and (often implausibly dramatic) ends, so the demands of narrative gratification are fulfilled episodically even as the main storyline of the community carries on interminably. Many examples of these communities are professional rather than domestic, being set in hospitals, police stations, or even, in the power-dressed days of the American 80s in the corporate world itself. In *Dallas* and *Dynasty* high drama was made partly out of boardroom intrigues. If soaps can turn to business, might the favour be returned for the task of Investor Relations with its episodic instalment the Annual Report?

I'm not suggesting that each Report should publish a yearly round-up of affairs, returns from the dead, arson plots and murders. This would be taking transparency a little too far. Yet there is much to learn from a genre that ultimately has the same purpose as Investor Relations: keeping its audiences with them. Everything about the open-ended, episodic machinery of the soap is focused on maintaining a relationship with its audience indefinitely. When successful this can breed obsession, with soap fans fiercely loyal to these characters and communities, and where the line between fiction and reality is delusionally thin.

Soap is a highly competitive business, with series engaging in a permanent ratings war, which, on the commercial channels translates directly into advertising and sponsorship revenue. The very name of the genre testifies to its close parity with the commercial world and the objectives of brand builders. FMCG manufacturers sought to tap into the devotion these long-term relationships nurtured, hoping to make their products as central to the lives of these audiences as were the dramas of the characters they followed. In a commercial soap, the most important character is really the brand that payrolls these dramas through sponsorship for as long as the audiences stay with them.

Such long-term commercial relationship-building is the purpose of Investor Relations. Its implicit message is stay with us, the story is going to get even better, the rewards for loyalty even more fulfilling. How can it do this? By building some of soap's episodic narrative momentum into its Reporting, and some of its human engagement into its long-term relationship-building. If a Report is considered an episodic instalment this will encourage its own narrative integrity as a compelling, coherent account of the year. The year end imposes closure, and so demands the storyteller's art to give that individual account meaning.

One way of achieving this is making Key Performance Indicators a stronger prominence in each yearly instalment. Performance defines the goal or Grail of ever-increasing value, a goal indefinitely deferred, but periodically gratified through major milestones and, of course, dividends. If this Grail shines enticingly at the end of the road both you and your investors are travelling, it is important to provide a clear map, coherent signposting, and progress reports. These are the milestones along the way, employing the rhythms of narrative gratification into the framework of financial returns. The more confident you are or wish to be perceived about the long-term journey, the more important it is to provide these milestones and maps. The Annual Report is partly an episodic progress report on that ongoing journey and its narrative. Its milestones give coherent shape to the open-ended investor-focused narrative the company is developing through time.

## To be continued...

In this way, individual storylines for that episode converge to form a coherent narrative for that year, contributing to the thread that binds past and future to the continuous present of the corporate community. Being clear about that core narrative of that community allows a company to identify these storylines, and bring greater coherence to both its annual reflections, and its ongoing projections and performance. An established company is a community after all. It has history (back story), and continuity of values and personnel, but is also subject to continuous evolution. New 'characters' join the cast, bringing with them their own back stories of experience and expertise. They make their own contributions to the company's story, either thriving as long-term stars who shape its narrative, or suffer the corporate equivalent of the soap's dramatic bumping off. The company adapts and evolves in response to challenges and opportunities in the world at large. Similarly, the slice-of-life realism of soap operas is a large part of their continuing appeal, drawing audiences in by reflecting the issues and dramas that touch their own lives. Annual Reports might usefully adopt a more slice-of-life focus too.

Explaining their business models means demonstrating clearly how the company's creation of value adds up to greater value in the wider world. What need in the wider world drives the challenges the company meets, the solutions it provides? How does it touch the world of people, issues and things? And as soap operas develop a very strong sense of place (*EastEnders* set in London; *Coronation Street* in Manchester; *Emmerdale* in rural Yorkshire), so Reports need to demonstrate their command of the specific marketplaces in which they operate. The more in touch with this market it shows itself to be, the more confidence it inspires, allowing investors to believe its story about this world is an accurate depiction.

As soap operas have more than their fair share of community-threatening catastrophes to contend with, so companies need to be far more transparent in acknowledging their risk profile, and far more coherent in their accounts of how they will tackle these issues. What creates drama in entertainment narratives, builds credibility in their corporate counterparts. But only if they are prepared to engage honestly with the world at large. Evidence of risk mitigation in action might be built into a case study, to show it is being taken seriously and translated into positive outcomes. This is not only more convincing than the compliance exercise of risk-listing, but employs the powerful dramatic formula of conflict overcome to positive effect (as suggested in the PowerPoint example earlier). Story demands dramatic incident, and the reward for honest acknowledgement of material risks is the credibility and trust born of narrative engagement and empathy.

A truly exemplary attempt to use storytelling to engage the investor community through difficult times is IBM's report from 2000. Instead of the usual reassuring platitudes adorning the cover, they decided to get straight to the heart of the matter, by summing up their year as if it were a rollicking read from the novel's earliest days. In mock eighteenth-century letterpress it grabbed corporate America's attention with the following:

"YOU'RE ONE PAGE AWAY
*from the* NO-HOLDS-BARRED STORY
*of* ONE YEAR
*in* THE LIFE OF A COMPANY.

*It's the story of*
BIG BATTLES,
STINGING DEFEATS
&
GRITTY COMEBACKS.
UNEXPECTED ALLIANCES,
DARING FORAYS
&
GAME-CHANGING
DISCOVERIES.

*in many ways,*
IT'S A STORY ABOUT THE FUTURE, AS WELL AS THE RECENT PAST,
AND ABOUT ALL BUSINESS TODAY.
WHICH MEANS IT'S ABOUT E-BUSINESS.
AND ONE IN PARTICULAR..."

It deserves to be a classic because it is modelled on one, or even many.

These were challenging times. The Internet bubble had burst, and all tech companies were guilty by association, or in very deep. And so, it confesses to 'stinging defeats', but also 'feisty comebacks', just like in the stories its audience grew up on. This is America, where the good guy usually wins. By self-consciously evoking, if not pastiching, both the verbal and visual rhetoric of storytelling, the company frames itself in the high heroic mode as a plucky survivor. It dug deep into the residual reserves of goodwill far more effectively than waffling away the disasters and making vague optimistic promises for the future.

The first chapter, entitled 'Reports of our Demise' appeared opposite a classic pulp fiction cover image of a boxer slugging his opponent out of the ring. This to illustrate IBM's "Feisty comebacks in servers, storage and databases". You've got to admire their pluck, if only their attempt to make that subject interesting. But comeback they did, IBM is not just a reinvented force to be reckoned with, it's also a seasoned storyteller. Its 'A Smarter Planet' initiative is a leading example of the trend for big brands to engage their audiences by publishing quality content, rather than just promoting products (more on this tendency in my final chapter). But as IBM's earlier foray into self-conscious narrative demonstrates, story is a great way of keeping your audiences rooting for you. If you approach reporting as an opportunity to open up and include people in your journey rather than an obligation to fulfil, you are more likely to keep them by your side. Through thick and thin.

Case studies provide perfect opportunities for narrative, and showing the business model in action. They have a core theme, because they should relate to a specific problem solved or issue resolved. They are completed, so have the beginning, middle and end of well-crafted narrative. If they show a problem solved there is scope to illustrate a need met, so there is every encouragement to bring out the human connection. And they demand the storyteller's skills of retrospective selection, simplification and conclusion. The messy stuff of day-to-day business practice can be shaped and crafted to illustrate a core competence, a lesson learned, a milestone achieved. Everything is in place for compelling storytelling. This section should really be the narrative centrepiece of every year's instalment. Yet how many companies really exploit case studies to their full potential? But, rather, have all the drama, risk, surprise or challenges drained out of them.

Each case study might be considered as a separate storyline showcasing the values and relevance of the wider corporate community and its story. Then consider these, like the most gripping soap opera storylines, reflective of the broader narrative and relevant to the world at large and the value-chain you participate in. These should be snapshots of the here and now of your story, the narratives with completion and closure yet part of the ongoing, open-ended narrative that keeps your relevance and relationship with your audiences alive. And as the famous cliff-hanger ensures audiences tune in for the next episode, well-crafted narrative at episodic level with a clear sense of how this is part of your long-term strategic 'plot', will help keep your own audiences expectantly engaged. The year end won't really be the end of your story, if you maintain a coherent ongoing dialogue through other communications channels throughout the year, nurturing the relationship as an open-ended, forward-focused narrative that keeps your audiences hooked.

Finally, as character identification is at the heart of soap opera success, companies might think more carefully about how they present their own 'casts'. Once again, there's a need to make it personal, encouraging the star cast of the corporate community and its story to come forward. To emerge as human beings from behind the stiff pictures and list-like CVs. Each cast member surely has his or her own story to contribute to the broader narrative, a defined role to play in the life of this community. What are those roles? What do they bring to the decision-making process, how is their experience relevant to the story you are telling? Can we hear this in their own voice, rather than the perfunctory third-person roll call of a company compelled to disclose who is in charge and (reluctantly) how much they are paid?

A company that has started to do this quite effectively is Pearson, the publishing and education business. It's not surprising that the owners of such brands as Penguin and the *Financial Times* might feel inclined to practice what they preach when it comes to storytelling. And so, their 2011 Annual Report is published as a video-rich PDF. It's really important for a company like Pearson to demonstrate that it is facing up to the challenges digital technology presents to its core publishing assets. You can say you are doing it, or you can more convincingly show you understand how people are accessing information or consuming stories by simply enhancing your own digital presence.

Which is what Pearson is doing. There are short videos about new acquisitions, animated presentations of key facts and figures. But most significantly, presentations and interviews showing board members and key executives personally explaining strategic intent and developments. It's difficult enough pinning important people down for even the photo shoot, let alone videos. So this shows a real commitment by a company who wants to explain where it is going and to bring people along with it.

Connecting as human beings, presenting developments in the true representative voice of a company will ultimately do more to inspire trust than the box-ticking, form-filling, detail-gathering disclosures of a legislation-compelled mindset. Create rapport rather than just 'report', and you will win the trust the corporate world so desperately needs to restore. Turning an obligation into an opportunity to build strong and meaningful relationships.

This may just come to pass if reporting takes hold of the communication advantages afforded by storytelling. Narrative Account, long-exiled through the ascendency of its Financial twin, may very well return to the reporting series. Will this dramatic story twist come about? The communications world eagerly awaits next year's exciting instalment…

# Through Sustainability Communications

The third item of the main list of new demands for reporting is to integrate financial with non-financial disclosures more effectively. With this in mind I have integrated my own chapters on Annual Reporting and Sustainability communications into a special 'omnibus edition'. The second part now focuses on how more coherent storytelling can help achieve greater integration between the two disciplines. In fact, through all disciplines, channels and communications.

Sustainability has traditionally been more accommodating to the idea of telling a story. Indeed, an *Economist* article from November 2004 entitled 'Corporate Storytelling' was all about 'Non-financial accounting', suggesting the concept of story entered business discourse through the CR backdoor. Emotive issues – people, rather than profit; melting icecaps rather than market caps – belong more readily to the 'softer' end of the communication spectrum. And yet, whilst many companies claim that Sustainability "informs everything we do", they tend to declare or support it in the designated pages of their website, or in a standalone report. Such partitioning undermines the statement in the very act of making of it. And if it is flatly contradicted by what goes on elsewhere, then it will convince, or inspire trust in nobody.

And so, what exactly is meant by 'integrated reporting', and how can this be achieved? Ben Richards, Head of Sustainability at Radley Yeldar provides an answer, first by explaining what it is not: "it isn't an Annual Report with a large Sustainability section. Nor is it an Annual Report with information tacked on at various points as an afterthought. Nor is it a report that tries to be all things to all people". OK. So what is it? "It's a report that seeks to show the relationship between financial and non-financial factors in a single narrative". Sounds good to me. But alarm bells start ringing as soon as I encounter a phrase like 'non-financial disclosure'. If 'disclosure' on its own indicates a mindset inhibitive to storytelling, the addition of an implied departure from the norm hints at the extent of the challenge before us. This challenge derives from historical legacies. Sustainability's own 'back story' means it starts from a very different perspective, and goes against the grain of its more hard-nosed counterpart.

I'm not talking about the politics of Sustainability, but the challenge of telling its story as part of a broader corporate narrative. Politics are partly the problem here. Whilst any company is free to tell its own story, explaining how it creates value and where it is going on its own terms, the Sustainability story belongs to everyone and is all about problems. It's shaped by the not-particularly welcome legacy of a lobbyist agenda historically at odds with the interests of the investor community. It is a collective story, dominated by attention-grabbing headlines which can be summed up simplistically and sensationally as 'we're all going to hell in a handcart if we don't act now'. A company's own contribution to this story is to explain what it is individually doing to mitigate (or perhaps even accelerate) this collective problem. This is where the problems start if alignment is the objective. Historically they start from different places, so their integration involves some resourceful strategic reorientation.

Here's the challenge as I see it. Put simplistically, and with the broadest of brush strokes, the main investor narrative is usually a story about *more*; the Sustainability story historically about *less*. The former about increasing (commercial, economic) impact; the latter about reducing (negative) impact. Investors and analysts have their eyes on the bottom line and a progressive narrative about what the company is doing to generate more value for shareholders. This is a given, a collective story too in a way, but one that goes entirely with the grain of its principal audience's interests. Growth is the Grail everyone is pursuing. It is then up to each individual company to make a compelling case through its personal story about why this archetypal narrative truly belongs to it. This is the implicit narrative of financial reporting, with everyone facing expectantly in the same direction *towards* the same goal of greater commercial impact leading to better financial returns.

Broadly speaking Sustainability starts from a different perspective and faces in the opposite direction. Its narrative imperative involves a company making a compelling case for what it is doing to mitigate the impact of its operations. Be this on the environment, on the welfare of communities or the welfare of its workforce. The very premise of mitigation means that its narrative momentum is *away* from problems, rather than *towards* opportunities. Not only is it facing in a different direction to the main investor story, it is going against the grain of narrative's natural inclinations.

## *Getting personal*

One of my themes is that stories love journeys, and feed off the human desire for progressive momentum. They don't thrive naturally when moving away from something. Even when the quest is to kill a monster or avert a catastrophe, the story is usually really about the growth of the hero through his journey to meet this threat. This holds good when they take on real issues, such as when Hollywood goes environmental. In the 2004 film *The Day After Tomorrow* the monster menacing New York City this time is no longer Godzilla or intergalactic aliens. It's the nemesis of environmental neglect in the form of the mother of all deep freezes. Yet the main storyline still involves the journey of an environmental scientist who prophesised all this into the very eye of the storm to rescue his estranged son. The journey is still a progressive and a deeply personal one. Cheesiness aside, it does once again suggest that the principles of storytelling as perfected by Hollywood are relevant even when dealing with the most serious challenges the world currently faces. That there is a need to be highly resourceful in tackling not only the challenges the Sustainability story identifies, but the challenges this story itself faces when seeking to integrate it more closely with the main corporate narrative.

There is every potential to do this. One of the major advantages of the term 'Sustainability' over the more paternalistic 'Corporate Social Responsibility', is its fitness for progressive narrative. Sustain is a verb, immediately signalling a commitment to do something, to go somewhere, to move towards a progressive goal. It is perfect for re-framing in terms of a goal-focused journey.

How? By once again learning from Hollywood, and personalising the political. If the Sustainability story belongs to lobbyists and headline makers, companies will always be playing 'bit parts' in someone else's epic. Everyone knows it matters; what companies need to explain is how it directly matters to their specific business. This isn't about speechifying on issues, but demonstrating how a company's individual Sustainability strategy reflects what is directly material to its core business or its brand. A good example of this in action is Reed Elsevier, the publishing company. Reed Elsevier's core product is information, which it sells to scientific, medical, legal, business and risk professionals. Central to its Sustainability activities is what it calls its 'Unique Contributions'. As it explains: "We believe we have the most significant impact when we apply our expertise to areas like universal, sustainable access to information, advancement of science and health, promotion of the rule of law and justice, and protection of society".

If knowledge is power, then a company like Reed Elsevier can have the most positive impact empowering those most in need of its expertise. Its case studies illustrate this by explaining how it is helping organisations tackle human trafficking through the dissemination of information; or how it is supporting medicine, agriculture or environmental initiatives in developing countries through free access to research and expertise. As expertise is what its brand is all about, Reed's efforts cumulatively reinforce its core story by demonstrating the global value of what it does. When the contributions you make are uniquely yours, then the story you tell can be too.

A material strategy can therefore reinforce a brand story, and also directly benefit the business. According to Ben, "material issues must go beyond the traditional comfort zone of measuring energy usage or community investment". These are the generic concerns that belong to the collective Sustainability story shaped by others. A bank convinces nobody by talking about local communities, or child labour (unless it's the Co-Op, of course); but if it has a robust approach to employee development and retention it is clearly showing how its policies impact its long-term competitive edge.

## *Getting real*

Materiality therefore provides a key opportunity to reassure even the most sceptical observers that by doing sustainable business a company is sustaining its own business. Ironically, because of the political origins of the Sustainability story, the more self-interested, even 'selfish', a company appears on the measures it is taking, the more convincing its story will appear. So a company should be crystal clear about how its approach to Sustainability brings it benefits. Whether it's generating revenue, reducing costs, managing risks or motivating the workforce, if the interests are aligned the narratives can be integrated. By entwining its own core business story and objectives with the Sustainability agenda, a company starts to personalise the political and take credible ownership of the issues. Personalising the Sustainability story in this way is the first step towards integrating financial with non-financial narratives.

A famous example of this strategic integration achieved by a UK company is Unilever. Before 2004 the FMCG giant was a classic House of Brands, finding no benefit in consumers knowing that the same company made many of the household brands they used, including those that competed for share of market in the same product categories. Since then it has increasingly reversed this policy, using the more consumer-friendly logo that signalled the company's relaunch in 2004 as a Branded House to endorse its products and add implied value to its diverse product range. From what the company declared back then, Sustainability issues were a major factor in encouraging it to step out from behind the corporate curtain: "The world we operate in is changing. Consumers are demanding more and more from the companies behind the brands, increasingly bringing their views as citizens into their buying decisions. They want brands they can trust... Standing visibly as Unilever behind our products will enable us to take the next step in transparency and accountability".

Its Sustainable Living Plan, launched in 2010, further commits to making Sustainability a core component of its main corporate narrative. Instead of the two narratives pulling in different directions they cohere to inform a balanced expression of strategic intent: "to *grow* the business while *reducing* our environmental footprint and *increasing* the positive contribution which we make to society" (my emphasis).

By recognising that sustainable business is in everyone's interests Unilever doesn't need to speak with a forked tongue. For as it declares: "in our experience, sustainability drives growth". Consumers want it; its customers and supply chain partners need to demonstrate it; and it encourages the company to innovate, thus giving it a competitive edge. Unilever can thus reconcile its ambition for growth with a strong focus on the positive impact of its core business.

Lifebuoy is one of its oldest brands, created to bring affordable sanitation to the disease-stricken populations of Victorian cities. It is now playing a similar role in parts of Asia, Africa and Latin America, where simple hygiene measures we in the West now take for granted, can make a major difference in different markets. The Lifebuoy Handwashing Behaviour Change Programme focuses on reducing respiratory infections and diarrhea, the world's two biggest causes of child mortality. By 2015 it aims to change the hygiene behaviours of 1 billion consumers by promoting its product. Now these initiatives are not soul-saving measures to balance its main business of pursuing profit. As it makes clear, these markets are highly attractive to the company, and constitute key opportunities for growth: "there are billions of people in the world who deserve the better quality of life products like soap, shampoo and clean drinking water can provide… we shouldn't be ashamed of growth". Sustainable growth, that is. Something you can only really claim if you have an integrated strategy, and an integrated business narrative.

Integrating narrative therefore starts with aligning objectives. If the core business story and the Sustainability strategy face in different directions and appear to want different things, then they will never be aligned. But if they seek to answer the same questions and achieve similar objectives, they will build a much stronger collective story. By joining forces and becoming a single narrative project, the core business story and the Sustainability story will trade-off some useful reciprocal benefits.

As I highlighted earlier, a listed company is now legally obliged to explain its business model, why what it does is part of a value-chain that touches the world at large. And if it wants to tell a more compelling, engaging, trust-enhancing story it has to get more emotional and reflect its human side far more prominently. The Sustainability story originates from that world at large, and deals with real, tangible and very pressing issues. It operates in the world of specifics, things, resources, and measurable impacts, rather than that elusive Grail everyone is pursuing, 'value'. The Unilever integrated narrative demonstrates such holistic thinking well, bringing consumers, interested communities and investors into the same frame of reference. The same story. As it implies, value doesn't flourish in a hermetically sealed environment governed exclusively by economics. It is connected to the purchasing decisions of consumers, who belong to communities and who are increasingly aware of their connected existence on an imperilled and deeply divided planet. Supply chain and value chain are intrinsically linked. Gaps in one create leaks in the other.

# Getting closer

Stories are a great way of showing the possibility of change without preaching, but only if they illustrate real, tangible and achievable outcomes. That's the strength of the parable, the issue-focused narrative demonstrating an implied course of action without explicitly telling people what to do. It's also partly why soap operas are useful not just for product sponsorship, but issue sponsorship too. Soap operas, especially in the UK, are very good at weaving real issues and problems from the world at large into their storylines. This helps maintain their claims to realism, but also makes big problems much more manageable through narrative development and resolution. Racism, homophobia, unemployment, financial crisis are taken from the headlines and woven into the fabric of everyday life which the narrative unpicks and then resolves.

Making Sustainability more personal for the corporate community normalises it, and makes the big problems it presents much more scalable, immediate and real. As each episode in a soap opera achieves resolution, so each individual case study supporting the main strategy marks a progressive achievement towards a defined, manageable and measurable objective. But those stories achieve little if they are not personally material to the core business, as grist to the corporate mill.

The political becomes the personal in a very real sense if a company's Sustainability story reflects the issues that are material and important to its people too. Employee welfare is, of course, an important part of developing a sustainable business. But employees are also essential when seeking to embed robust Sustainability within the culture of an organisation. As Ben puts it: "Sustainability issues often resonate with individual's personal beliefs. They can inspire people within an organisation to be part of its story if that story involves aspects other than simply making money". Sustainability becomes a collective objective and a more convincing story if this story is personalised and shared. Asking questions such as "what does it mean to me, my team, for all of us"? broadens the ownership of initiatives, and becomes a chorus rather than a managerial monologue on issues outside of most people's reach.

This is again partly about using storytelling to bring big things down to a human scale. The Big Sustainability Story of the headlines (especially the environmental headline-grabber) is about colossal problems that get bigger and more remote with every fresh report. Too big for any one company or even one country to deal with, and a story without any foreseeable closure (bar that of global catastrophe). Individual stories about Sustainability issues make big problems human sized, bring them closer to every day life, and allow the possibility of individual plot resolutions. They seem less impossible as a consequence, and can be a tangible expression of a company's values to both external and internal audiences alike.

Which brings me to the next important place to tell a corporate story: internally.

# Through your People

Here I talk all about Employee Engagement, or what is sometimes called Internal Communications. Story has a major role to play here because it is all about people. Not figures, results, strategies, visions, values or messages, but people. Diligent, dedicated, valuable, voluble, independent, insecure, disgruntled, disengaged, uncontrollable people. The 'greatest asset' of many organisations (or so they claim) as well as the biggest liability if they don't feel this is true. Corporate storytelling would be a relatively simple matter were it not for people.

You can craft your core story down to a nicety, employing the full panoply of narrative principles until you have the very Booker prize of corporate comms. But if the story you tell and the reality that is experienced don't match up, then your story will be just that, a story. A lie in fact. With a service or B2B brand this is largely determined by how employees and representative behave, or the personal relationships they build. As Wally Olins has observed, in such cases "the most important audience for the organization is its own people". If a corporate story told through communications is a surrogate for the journey you want to take customers on, then this is where that journey gets real. The narrative buck stops here.

But it starts here too. If people are the ultimate problem here they are also the solution. Story is the most human-centric mode of communication we have. Because it ultimately resides in the hearts and imaginations of recipients, people are the true media of its truths. By helping to establish belief and belonging internally, story provides the master key for engaging the collection of individuals that make up an organisation. Belief and belonging are among the fundamental drivers of the human urge for narrative, and can help encourage desired behaviour by tapping into the powerful forces that have shaped our collective existence as a species.

# *Belief*

The success of any story in any context depends in a large part on its believability. Even the wildest fictional fantasies have to remain plausible within the bounds they establish. Explaining the Whys and ways of the world is one of the most ancient functions of story. Such wisdom is the bedrock of belief, as understanding *that* things happen in predictable ways is a prelude to explaining *why?* The Whys of the empirical world can build communities of belief through narrative. For, as Brian Boyd points out, "religious convictions derive less from doctrine than from story". The empirical can slide into the ethical if you have a master narrative explaining Why. Someone or something in charge. Belief becomes a potent cohesive and regulatory principle for any community, shaping its sense of where it has come from, how it should act and where it is going. Such belief can carry it through the wilderness years, and keep it focused on its destiny in a Land of Milk and Honey. Belief can move mountains, if the story enshrining this belief is compelling enough.

Humans are not particularly good at change. Yet the business world feeds on it, restlessly searching for new roads to riches, new worlds to conquer. Stories are also always about change. They introduce conflict to create dramatic interest, and build narrative momentum by resolving the problems they create. Whilst humans might resist imposed or unexplained change, they do like and need stories. It's also likely that their own stories of selfhood involve personal goals, aspirations and journeys. We rule our lives through the stories we tell ourselves. About who we are, where we've come from, and where we believe we are heading. Employee is only one role we play in the complex dramas of our lives. Life is constantly throwing us experiences that we make sense of in terms of stories (memories, anecdotes, gossip). And we are constantly presented with stories that teach us all about life. Both aspects of storytelling are relevant in this context, with narrative providing a bridge between resistant individuals and insistent businesses.

Using story to affect change is what Stephen Denning's famous concept of 'The Springboard Story' is all about. As he explains:

"A springboard story is a story that enables a leap in understanding by the audience so as to grasp how an organization or community or complex system may change. A springboard story has an impact not so much through transferring large amounts of information, but through catalyzing understanding. It enables listeners to visualize from a story in one context what is involved in a large-scale transformation in an analogous context".

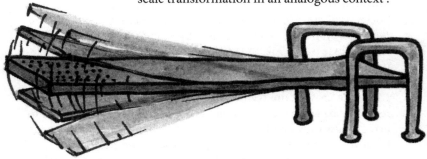

Such stories help leaders to bring about organisational change, and overcome resistance by appealing to the heart and imagination, rather than providing a whole load of rational justifications. Stories enable people to picture the future in inspirational ways, and see themselves as part of it. Inspire first, justify second; working back from the vision of changed realities with the steps that will take you there. For, as Denning points out: "Anyone who has a new idea and wants to change the world will do better telling stories than by offering any number of reasons". Visionaries, messiahs and inspirational demagogues repeatedly illustrate this through history. The future is always envisaged through stories (both utopian and dystopian), and can provide 'springboards' into new realities through narrative.

If your own story isn't inspiring enough, you can always borrow one. Not from a competitor or as a 'me too' bid to be something you are not, but from the great story archive we all carry around with us in our collective memory. Peter Guber's book *Tell To Win* opens with a personal story about how he discovered the power of storytelling in a commercial context. Guber was a successful movie exec, whose company Columbia Pictures Entertainment was acquired by Sony in 1989. Gruber found himself CEO of a sinking, demoralised ship. His team lacked direction and any sense of belonging to an organisation "7,000 miles and a major culture gap away". But Guber casts himself as a hero, determined to find a "creative way to persuade both Sony and the disparate, disgruntled band of executives I'd inherited to unite and play for the future. But how?"

Through inspirational storytelling, of course. They were in the business of stories, after all, and so Guber seized on the tale of *Lawrence of Arabia*, as immortalised by Peter O'Toole in Columbia's iconic movie from 1962. In 1917 Lawrence attempted the impossible, uniting a disparate band of Arab tribes to attack a Turkish garrison defending its hold on Arabia at the now Jordanian port of Aqaba. Lawrence crossed the Nefud desert, believed to be impassable, to reach Aqaba while the Turks defended the sea. His success helped to bring a measure of unity among the Arabs, and expel the Ottoman's from the region. It created a legend, was made into a film, and then a succinct mythical formula applied to a similarly impossible situation in early 90s Tinsletown. Guber distributed framed photos of O'Toole as Lawrence to all his execs, drew the analogy and only had to intone the rallying cry 'Aqaba' whenever their resolve faltered. The rest, according to Guber's heroic retelling, is Hollywood history.

People respond to and participate in stories only when can find their relevance to their own personal narratives. Which is why something like 'maximising shareholder value' is not a story, or really even the makings of one. Those tasked with delivering this will want something a bit more inspiring and personally relevant if they are to help it come to pass. Participation through personal recognition is essential in this context. For, as Radley Yeldar's Isabel Collins, explains, employees are unique "in that they are both actors and audiences in the story's performance. This makes them arguably the most important and most critical audience in the equation". Critical in all senses. If they don't buy it, they won't buy into it, and so will not play the role scripted for them.

The big inspirational narratives have an important role to play in ensuring people understand the vision, and sign up for the journey towards it. But these visions are nearly always utopian, and cannot be sustained indefinitely if they are not reinforced by narratives that connect directly with the individual actors' roles in the collective drama. This is where individual stories have a role to play in supporting the vast span of the corporate or visionary narrative, which can collapse if it is not grounded in the daily reality of those tasked with delivering it.

Narrative brings things to life, making them tangible and relevant. This applies to specific issues as much as abstract ideals or motivating visions. The importance of health and safety or security vigilance is far more effectively understood and internalised through story. A code of conduct, or a list of rules is impossible to remember, and is far too dry or seemingly remote for most people who just want to get on with their jobs. Such documents usually dwell on 'What' – what's expected of people – whereas 'Why' this ultimately matters is vital for building belief and affecting change. Story is great for explaining Why. It places issues in context and shows the consequences of actions through narrative. Stories illustrate the relationships between things, allowing people to see the bigger picture, and understand their own role within it.

Showing the bigger picture through storytelling was the objective of a series of safety films Radley Yeldar made for Network Rail. Network Rail is responsible for operating and maintaining the infrastructure and systems of Britain's rail network.

Safety is, of course, of paramount importance, and so there is always a need to reinforce its principles throughout the whole organisation. For this network to operate efficiently it's essential that an holistic view is taken, where people don't just think about their own or their team's role, but how what they do can have a knock on effect down the line.

The company commissioned a series of short films to promote such 'System Safety' thinking. This encouraged us to suggest breaking with the usual genre. A genre my colleague in Employee Engagement, Martin Skeet, calls "ketchup on the tracks". As he explains, safety films tend to depict "something bad happening, and then draw the lesson from this about what you shouldn't do". They tend to be quite didactic. And so, because someone got it wrong, the defensive barriers can go up in the audiences, who might unconsciously resent an implied finger wagging. Such gruesome spectacles can also use up the experience in emotion, repelling people but leaving little room for the learning they are designed to convey.

So to break with the genre, Martin and his team suggested using humour, and a very different style to the usual slice-of-life melodramas. Humour can deal with difficult issues, but it can also break down barriers, and put people in a more receptive frame of mind. Celebrating what people did right encourages others to identify with the 'hero', thus reinforcing behaviour in a positive engaging way. To encourage this identification they used animation. Animation, as I suggested earlier, is great for universalising. In a complex, multi-faceted system such as a rail network, it's vitally important that people do not think too locally. Realistic footage runs the risk of people focusing on the specifics rather than the bigger issue at hand: thinking "that's not my region, that's not my problem".

So, the team created an illustrated diagram of the entire network, which they then brought to life through a series of animated incidents. A whole world was created, a bit like a 2-D Trumpton (yes, I'm very old), with each episode narrating a different incident somewhere in this big but connected world. These incidents were not Toy Town fantasies 'though. Each story was based upon real anecdotes and incidents gathered through consultation with people from controllers to trackside personnel.

My favourite is about a cow on the track, and how a potentially network-closing incident was averted by Dave the switched-on controller doing the right thing. The story literally reverses expectations, putting surprise to good effect by telling the story twice, with two different endings. The first depicts what might have happened, the potential threat to the system that reinforces the need for joined-up, System Safety thinking. The action then goes into reverse, and replays what actually happened, catastrophe (not to mention the usual sombre didacticism) averted with a happy ending. Using comedy rather than tragedy meant that professionalism could be celebrated, shared and reinforced.

Real anecdotes and incidents could be circulated around the entire network through these films, building a community through storytelling, whilst encouraging bigger-picture thinking by means of a pooping animated cow.

## *Belonging*

Belief is only one part of the equation for engaging internal audiences through story. It is incomplete without the emotional connection born of belonging. Belonging is another fundamental function and outcome of story, pointing to the role of narrative in tribal bonding. Sharing a common story powerfully brings a disparate group of individuals together to share common values and pursue common goals. As Jonathan Gottschall points out in his fascinating book *The Storytelling Animal*, the tribal function of storytelling goes very deep. He even suggests the rather counterintuitive, if not heretical, view (if you are Richard Dawkins) that religion may serve an evolutionary function enabled by sacred narrative. Bringing people together around a common code of belief and values can encourage cooperative behaviour vital to the survival of the tribe.

Stories don't just reflect reality, they reinforce behavioural norms, creating cooperative communities bonded by ethical standards. Before writing, this could only be imparted orally, and narrative is the most effective means of ensuring messages live in the imagination and stick in the memory. Think of gossip, the most everyday manifestation of the human need to tell stories. As gossip circulates, so it regulates, sustaining tacit behavioural norms through the exchange of anecdote. Gossip, is of course, endemic in the corporate environment, a culture primed for using storytelling to far more constructive effect.

Sharing a story reinforces its ability to both move and bond individuals. As Gottschall reminds us, until relatively recently storytelling was predominantly a communal, performative activity: "For uncounted millennia, story was exclusively oral. A teller or actor attracted an audience, synced them up mentally and emotionally, and exposed them all to the same message". Stories still have this potential. Gottschall prescribes a cinema visit to see this in action. Not to watch the movie, but the audience: "If the movie is good, the people will respond to it like a single organism. They will flinch together, gasp together, roar with laughter together, choke up together. A film takes a motley association of strangers and syncs them up. It choreographs how they feel and what they think ... Until the lights come up and the credits roll, a film makes people one".

Making the many one – believing as one, belonging as one, behaving as one – is, of course gold dust for anyone seeking to influence a body of individuals. This is why propagandists find stories (as well as public rallies) far more effective than simply disseminating doctrine. Yet this influence needn't be manipulative or malign, and can be used to simply ensure a corporate lives up to its name, and acts more purposefully as one body. Now, I'm not talking about creating lobotomised corporate clones. Quite the opposite. The unique power of stories is their ability to both individualise and universalise. By appealing to a common humanity, people are able to recognise their own selves and stories within broader narratives and step into the collective circle.

The very act of sharing individual stories can bring people together, as any campfire moment demonstrates. This is one of the main roles of narrative in the corporate setting for professional storytellers such as Annette Simmons, who proposes it as a far more effective and long-lasting people fixative than such ephemeral team-building stunts as white-water rafting or paintballing. Whilst these are immediately focused on action, humans are more likely to act as a community if they have things in common, and remember those things long after the adrenalin-stoked camaraderie has faded along with the stains and the bruises. Story gets to the heart of this commonality. Not only is it a powerful 'choreographer' of emotions as an experience, it is a powerful connector of human beings through the recognition of common experiences and values. The sharing of stories can serve a bonding role in its own right (a form of narrative grooming for besuited primates). But it also yields insights that contribute to the collective narrative lore of an organisation, providing anecdotal evidence of shared values, beliefs and goals.

Such connection is particularly useful when there is a need to erode entrenched divisions and silos within an organisation. Humans are fundamentally tribal animals, something that can work for good or ill, depending on where their allegiances reside. The tribal sentiment which narrative nurtures can also encourage divisiveness and foster cynicism if the centre of belonging is too locally focused. A sense of 'Us' is nearly always reliant on a 'Them'. That's fine if 'Them' are the competition, as a common enemy is a great way of unifying a tribe. Yet too often this focus fragments internally, with the principal 'Them' being another team within a division, another division on the same floor, another region, a recently acquired company, or those high up in the C-Suite who believe they are steering a happy ship all pulling in the same direction.

If the big story a company tells has no relevance or resonance for individuals or their tribes, these individuals are likely to subscribe to more localised narratives that undermine and fragment the official one. They will carry their own firmly held stories of grievance or indifference around with them, and you have to work hard to replace this with your own story. But you need to listen to those stories first. Individual stories, or stories belonging to a team, can provide a bridge between the personal and the collective. The big corporate story might appear too abstract and remote, without such intermediary narratives establishing connections. The individual story contributes to the team narrative, which in turn can find points of connection with the collective corporate narrative, and build a robust framework for belief and belonging.

A particularly acute need for such 'narrative engineering' is when there has been a merger or acquisition. It's hardly surprising that the alliance of two formerly warring tribes might not be an immediate recipe for communal bliss. An acquired/merged company may lose its name, move to new premises, be subsumed within an apparently indifferent entity, but you can be sure collective identity will remain through the stories it tells itself. Stories helped keep the Children of Israel together through the centuries of captivity and exile. "Yea, we wept, when we remembered Zion". They can do the same in what might feel like exile in a new company, perpetuating fragmentation and dissent.

Such tribal lore can be turned to positive account if it is given space and makes its contribution. No doubt the new parent paid a lot for the company, it may as well use the stories not featured on the corporate lawyers balance sheets, but which in the long term may make all the difference. Listen to these stories. Let them make their contribution. "We do things differently". Great. Explain how. If such anecdotes become part of the collective lore of the company – through case studies, insights, a new values set – then it is more likely that the two tribes will start to become one, and set their warring sights on a new common enemy residing two steel and glass encampments along.

Collect, Celebrate, Circulate should be the mantra for a corporate storytelling culture. Not broadcast. The many are more likely to become the one, if the many (stories) support and feed into the one, rather than vice versa. A corporate story built from the ground up is far more likely to bear the weight of its ambition, and brave the tempests of circumstance. The plurality of stories is a strength to be celebrated rather than heresy to be suppressed, and goes with the grain of how storytelling is developing in the broader communications landscape.

As will be explored shortly, developments in digital media have started to erode established distinctions between internal and external, brand owner and brand audience. Social media externally finds its counterpart internally in the form of 'Social Enterprise' platforms such as Yammer, which are increasingly replacing intranets for circulating information internally. The more fluid exchanges people have come to take for granted through their external networks draw attention to the limitations of the more top-down, command and control mode of communication within. Platforms such as Yammer are great for allowing the horizontal flow of ideas to find collective solutions to corporate needs, and for empowering individual 'actors' in the collective corporate production. And, like their counterparts externally are perfect for circulating and celebrating people's stories.

Such sharing is particularly appropriate when it comes to the issue of corporate 'Values'. Most companies have a set of values. They often list them, sometimes explain them, and occasionally live by them. A way of connecting people more closely to a company through values, is asking them what they value about the company. This can help align personal value sets with the corporate ones, allowing people to recognise and 'own' them as personally relevant. It's also likely to generate stories when you ask for examples of these values in action. These might not always be the ones it officially proclaims, as I recently had occasion to witness.

A company was pretty clear about what its corporate values were, and engaged us to help disseminate them through communications. We conducted a series of workshops designed to gather individual stories that demonstrated these agreed values in action. Yet what we discovered was a mine of anecdotes that consistently pointed to a different, more distinctive, more authentic set of values than the ones agreed in advance, and which reflected how the company felt it ought to be perceived. These revelations at first created something of a crisis; but the exec eventually recognised a truer reflection of itself in these authentic stories. Gathering and sharing the stories that reflected its values had a greater longer-term value than the communications tasked with circulating them. The company found its true self through narrative.

Companies don't have values. People do. A company that celebrates and circulates its people's stories demonstrating values at work creates a much more credible and cohesive sense of belonging than one that advertises adjectives paired with clip art around the office walls. Adjectives remain abstractions without real stories to illustrate them. 'Performance' is not something you talk about, it is something you demonstrate. That goes for Integrity, Teamwork, Customer focus, and all the usual words companies intone in the hope that such incantatory rhetoric will magically make it true.

Words do have magic. They cast their spell more powerfully when they are formed into stories, and are more convincing and influential when those stories are true.

# Through the Digital Universe

The web is a foreign country. They do things differently there. I'm advised to remember this every time I work on a digital project. The rules are constantly being rewritten. The status quo is perpetual revolution. Multiple platforms, micro-segmentation of users, audience empowerment through social media, all potentially lead to fragmentation of story, dilution of brand. The old push model of corporate monologue won't wash. Users want to pull in content where and when they want it, tailored to their needs, answerable to their views, from sources they trust. They are 'always on', on the move and have little time and even less patience. If it's not real-time and relevant, adaptive to their devices you've lost them. What role can storytelling – perfected in literary and cinematic media, and associated with the broadcast mindset of traditional marketing – play in this topsy turvy, constantly moving, audience empowered world? Must we totally rethink everything that has gone before?

Not entirely. Whilst we shouldn't expect the old-world means and methods to slot neatly into these new channels and circumstances, we shouldn't be so overawed by the differences or so overwhelmed by the technology, that we lose sight of the common denominator surviving into even these turbulent times: human nature. As long as it is human beings who are creating and participating in digital experiences there will be a role for story. We just need to be more resourceful about how its principles are applied. Even more clear, more coherent, and especially more connected.

# Standing out

If the first principle of story is clarity, then this couldn't be more needed here. Online content creation cries out for the discipline of storytelling. Pare it down. Signpost it clearly. Cut out the jargon. Manage the details. Keep lines and paragraphs short, with one idea per paragraph. As users scan rather than consume content, you have to be extra vigilant to ensure they cannot miss the point, obscured by a wall of waffle or buried deep in some dungeon of detail. Web users are a peculiarly impatient species, we are told. They are trying to do a thousand things at once, and are besieged by distractions. You are merely one possible source for what they are looking for. They will devote very little time to looking for it. Attention, it would appear, is at a premium online.

Attention, according to Brian Boyd, is also a major psychological component of storytelling. Whilst it might be in particularly urgent need now, it has also played a key role in our evolution as a species. As his *On the Origin of Stories* explains, the old social Darwinist view that evolution rewards selfishness has been largely rejected, with evolutionists now stressing the adaptive advantages of cooperation within a social unit. However individuals still need to compete within these units. For resources, but also for maternal love. As Boyd puts it, "The more dominant the primate, the more attention others direct towards him or her". And he references the inordinate amount of attention the media still bestows upon the rich and famous as a measure of their success. But he also explains how storytelling has attention-grabbing and gratifying built into its very machinery: "We crave acceptance and, if possible, respect, prestige and status because of the difference they can make. Since the attention art can command offers both a first payout of status and a base for latter dividends, artists can be strongly driven by the desire for wide, high or long-lasting attention".

The bard, the jester, the stand-up comedian, and the class clown all find a route to preferment in the attention-grabbing dynamics of storytelling. If story can keep a drowsy (and despotic) emperor awake above the uproar of his court, it can surely work on impatient analysts and journalists on a crowded tube train. Whilst there may not be time to ask "are you sitting comfortably"? the means to grab attention and hold an audience have been perfected through millennia of narrative practice.

If the corporate website is a window on your world, it needs to be kept crystal clear, with your story prominently displayed for immediate standout. Video is a great way for achieving this online. For once I'll briefly bombard you with some facts and statistics, as these particular stats are quite attention grabbing in their own right.

Research found that web pages that include video have a fifty percent better chance of appearing on the first page of a Google search, and deliver a higher click-through rate as the content really stands out in text-based results lists. The advantage starts with Google's optimising richer content. Video pulls us in.

Another study found that whilst ninety percent of internet users leave a text site in four seconds, sixty percent leave in that time if video is on the home page. The same study found that visitors who remain linger for an average of five minutes and fifty seconds on a site featuring video, as opposed to forty-two seconds for a text-based site. Video keeps us there too.

We're not talking YouTube yoofs looking for performing pets here. *Forbes Magazine* surveyed US corporate executives about their online habits, and found that nearly sixty percent of their survey said they would watch video before reading text on the same web page. And seventy-five percent watch work-related video on business websites at least once a week. Twenty-six percent watch website business video daily. Video brings us back for more. *Forbes* also found that sixty-five percent of their survey had visited a vendor's website after watching a video hosted elsewhere; whilst fifty-three percent have conducted a search to locate more information. Moving Image moves us to act too.

Of course, there's video and there's video. Whilst this is obviously a popular medium for engaging audiences online, the gnat-like attention of web users demands that you have to gratify what you have grabbed. Fifty-three percent of viewers click away from online video within one minute. So, either the videos hosted need to be brutally succinct, or so irresistibly compelling and well-crafted that they convert clickers away into stickers around, gratifying the attention you've grabbed with a clear and coherent narrative experience.

And that's where the challenges really start.

## *Joining up*

As everyone knows, stories are supposed to have beginnings, middles and ends. Even the films of David Lynch or Tarantino, who push sequential narrative to the limits, eventually throw their audiences a line. A thread is there to be found if we are prepared to search for it. But online audiences probably aren't. You can't control the beginnings and middles of web journeys, let alone the ends. The beginning is where the user joins it (which could be anywhere if they've Googled in), and the end is when they say it is. The middle will be very short if they can't navigate swiftly and smoothly to what they need. Coherence, as I've argued, is essential for turning otherwise random messages into a story. Yet randomness is what the web is all about.

The discipline of User Experience (UX) has evolved specifically to answer this need. And as the following succinct description suggests, UX might simply be considered web jargon for storytelling:

"A user journey is a path a user may take to reach their goal when using a particular website. User journeys are used in designing websites to identify the different ways to enable the user to achieve their goal as quickly as possible". (Experience Solutions.co.uk).

Apart from the final reference to speed, this definition would serve perfectly well for the concept of 'throughline' essential to the fictional and dramatic arts. Entertainment stories use a character's throughline as their goal and motivating purpose, they then put obstacles in their path to create the conflict upon which drama thrives. UX is also about character development, relying on archetypal 'personae' to ensure core user demographics achieve their objectives. These characters, like their fictional counterparts, have back stories, names, ambitions, hobbies and obsessions, but above all goals. Then different scenarios are scripted to ensure these characters reach their goals under various circumstances.

In UX individual web pages are considered "decision points that carry the user from one step to another". Decisions are what fictional characters and website users take on their journeys. Narrative, as I've argued, is a problem-solving mechanism. And this applies to functionality as much as to fun. In entertainment stories the structured journey is an end in itself. In online communications it is an efficient means to a defined end. UX ponders the same questions as storytellers – of motivation, direction and context – to create coherent narrative journeys.

That's the theory. Yet even if users don't stick rigidly to the UX plot, like audiences of Tarantino or Lynch, they might just create narrative order themselves. The human brain likes to make connections and find patterns, and gains pleasure from solving problems. Remember the sage advice of the screenwriter that films should give audiences 2 + 2 rather than 4? Online you probably can't give them 4 directly anyway. But users might just piece together 2 + 2, or even 1 + 1 + 1 + 1. Yet only if the content is compelling, and the website functions as a storytelling channel, a showcase for the individual stories that engage audiences with your core brand narrative. This, of course, starts with a clear idea what that story is, which then informs editorial policy on what content supports it with on-the-ground examples. A corporate website can serve as a live storytelling feed, connecting with audiences, through real, relevant and timely stories about what you do and why it matters.

I was recently involved in a project that had this principle at the centre of the brief. GlaxoSmithKline (GSK), the global healthcare company, wanted to redesign its corporate website. This had outgrown its origins and needed to move to a Content Management System. The CMS would allow the company to rethink its online communication priorities, whilst a more adaptable interface design would mean it could share its story in more engaging ways with all its stakeholders. GSK already had a great story, defined by its mission: "to improve the quality of human life by enabling people to do more, feel better and live longer".

Yet GSK is a complex organisation, driven by scientific research and development, and ultimately answerable to its shareholders. The need to connect what might be going on in the lab (such as a breakthrough vaccine in the late stages of tests), with the knowledge-hungry demands of the investment community, often meant the human impact stories about why they do this got buried too many layers down. Factor in GSK's ownership of consumer healthcare brands such as *Ribena*, *Lucozade* and *Panadol*, and you have a diverse mix of audiences and messages to bring together in one place.

We thought the "Do More. Feel Better. Live Longer." strapline could help here, by doing a lot more itself. So we proposed using it as the narrative thread connecting the stories GSK showcased online. There was a wealth of great potential stories, but the website had outgrown its Information Architecture, meaning higher-value and impact content was often buried. The great stories needed to reach the surface. And so, while we ensured the investment and scientific communities, journalists and career seekers could easily access the information they sought, we also wanted the site to provide a more immersive experience in the company's narrative.

GSK's core story was relevant to all those audiences, and so we designed a prominent section of the homepage which invited all users to 'Explore GSK'. This opened a window on GSK's world by explaining their impact around the globe. The mix of stories showed the breadth of their operations, across pharmaceutical, vaccine and consumer healthcare, but with Doing More, Feeling Better, Living Longer providing the theme and focus for what this all added up to. This thread was woven consistently through the site architecture, ensuring wherever you were, and however you got there, you understood what GSK was all about. By inviting users to explore GSK's story about life, we brought their own story to life online.

# *Joining in*

With compelling content clearly displayed, and coherent user journeys, a corporate website can be a great place for companies to tell their stories. But is this what online audiences are looking for? Are they not principally looking for information? If your story gets in the way of that need, then it will have precisely the opposite effect it was designed to have. And a corporate site may actually be the last place people now go to access the information they need, relying on their networks, third-party forums or blogs before seeing what the company itself has to say. For story to survive and thrive online it has to adapt to customs of the country. Content may still be king, but it is reduced to a constitutional monarch in these democratised times. It has to work closely with first minister Context, and is ultimately answerable to new power in the realm: the User.

Users are on the move, always on, and expect content to scale to their devices and adapt to their needs. Demanding "Great content spread through social media and consumed anywhere", as one recent report on digital marketing trends summed it up. One-size-fits-all won't wash anymore. Design needs to be adaptive, allowing content to flow to different devices, and scale to different contexts – desktop or laptop, tablet, smartphone or traditional phone; at work, on the move or at home. Content owners now need to author once and publish many times, and can no longer see the corporate website as the central broadcasting hub. Broadcast is no longer tenable, as users increasingly demand far more tailored content, depending on their circumstances and preferences. They don't want stuff pushed at them, but want to pull in what they are looking for.

And who are these 'users'? Do they really conform to the categories of Investors, Media, Careers, Corporate, or Customers we've traditionally labelled them with? Such labels might make content creation and management easier for companies, but do not necessarily reflect the way users access information. On any given day, a business customer might also be a potential investor, a potential employee, or a consumer of the product or service. And then next day it's all change. So it's better to think of mindsets and behaviours rather than such rigid and internally-focused designations, when adapting content to audience. A 'Dater Miner' one day may be a 'Rapid Reader' the next, or grow into a 'Brand Ambassador' through time. Really understanding the mindsets and behaviours of users, demands a more human-centric approach to communicating. The more the user is in the ascendant, the more channel owners have to subordinate their own communication objectives to the demands and habits of individual users, the more they have to rethink how they attempt to tell their story online.

If mobility of users is creating the need for a new way to share content, adapted to their restless habits and precise demands, then this potentially turns the journey metaphor for stories on its head. By making it real. In the relatively 'passive' media of print, screen or stage, involvement is achieved through empathy. Audiences imaginatively put themselves in the protagonist's shoes, and are moved to understand the message or moral of the story by this emotional connection. The story 'transports' audiences. The storyteller takes people with them, if only in imagination. In this new mobile media environment, audiences actually are on a journey. It's their say whether you are allowed to accompany them. And so it's down to you to keep up with them, shaping your story to the journey they are on. The roles and relationships are reversing. The user doesn't identify with the hero. He or she is the hero, engaging with the content, being part of the story, going on the never-ending journey in real-time.

## *Letting go*

The technological revolution has achieved what all revolutions, by definition, eventually accomplish. It has come full circle. The touch screen environment symbolised by the tablet (and tablets of clay or wax were one of the earliest media for written communication), puts a premium on manual dexterity as of no time since perhaps when primates first evolved elongated opposable thumbs and gained technological mastery of their world. It is happening again in the virtual world of information and the machinery of its dissemination. Digital technology is now quite literally that, as the humble finger becomes the preferred tool of the tuned-in info seeker on his or her joined-up journey through the day. Technology has made itself invisible, and shaped itself intuitively to human form. Humanity is back on top, and steadily wresting control of the media once preserved for the few, to tell its own stories. We have moved through a communications cycle: from oral to written; written to technologically-restricted reproduction and dissemination by the few to the many; to the technologically-enabled sharing of the many with the many.

In April 1999, when the corporate world was preparing for the Y2K time bomb that never exploded, a band of disruptive web visionaries identified an incendiary quietly ticking away that finally has. *The Cluetrain Manifesto* consisted of 95 theses about how the internet was developing and what this might ultimately mean for businesses and their audiences. It claimed to be "lobbing bombs", but also "optimistic" about what it foresaw. It spoke of conversations, connections, a human-centric web, and networks as "markets" which operated like the physical marketplaces of old, where people met, exchanged stories, traded gossip and ideas as much as goods. One thesis stated that: "People in networked markets have figured out that they get far better information and support from each other than from vendors. So much for corporate rhetoric about adding value to commoditized products". In this, and other prescient proclamations The Cluetrain has finally delivered.

If this were only a technological revolution it would not have mobilised so many people. It would not have created such a groundswell. 'The groundswell' is the term Charlene Li and Josh Bernoff use to describe this massive upsurge in peer-to-peer networking. And to those who would seek to pitch their marketing tent in this avalanche of consumer empowerment they issue the following challenge: "Start by admitting that you are no longer in charge... Your brand is whatever your customers say it is. And in the groundswell where they communicate with each other, they decide". A brand has always been what customers say it is. It's just that until recently those customers' ability to broadcast *their* views about the brand has been relatively restricted.

Not any more.

# The End?

"There are millions of threads in this conversation,
but at the end of each one is a human being. That this
world is digital or electronic is not the point.
What matters most is that it exists in
narrative. *The story has come unbound*".
*The Cluetrain Manifesto*

# chapter five
# Where Story is going

––

The empowerment of individuals, pre-eminently through social media and networking, is potentially eroding distinctions – between internal and external, audience and author, brand owner and brand consumer – that have traditionally defined communications practice. How these developments affect storytelling and the principles I've so earnestly elaborated, I will now consider in this, the denouement of my story. This involves revisiting my model for the storytelling landscape I introduced in the first section, to consider what impact emergent trends might have on the future of corporate storytelling.

# The landscape of storytelling revisited

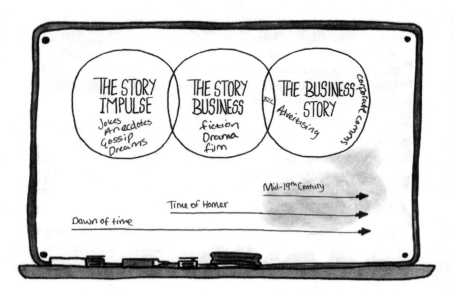

I envisaged the landscape of storytelling involving three interlocking spheres arranged as a spectrum. At one extreme is what I have called the *Story Impulse*. This contains the everyday world of storytelling most humans participate in naturally, even unconsciously, every single day. This is storytelling at its most basic and informal, with roots deep into the origins of our species. Gossip is the most representative form of storytelling belonging to this sphere.

The second sphere, which I've entitled the *Story Business,* is far more structured and professional. It employs story as a conscious practice, applying the craft of narrative to exploit for pleasure and profit the same impulses found in the first sphere. Whilst we know its stories are not true, we still welcome and actively seek them out. Any form of fiction, be it literary, cinematic, or dramatic, characterises storytelling in this sphere.

The third sphere I've called the *Business Story*. This contains all the arts of communication in the service of commerce or administration. Despite its high professionalism it is only semi-structured in its storytelling, low on credibility and acceptance. Ironically, despite its claims to veracity, people are less ready to believe the stories issuing from this sphere than the fictions coming from the second, which appeal to the truth of human nature. Jargon is its characteristic form, which signals its self-imposed isolation from the first sphere. Paradoxically, these are the people it ultimately depends on, to sell its stuff or services to. Sphere number three desperately needs sphere number one to trust it more.

I suggested that the way for this third sphere to gain the trust of the first was to consciously adopt some of the principles of the second. By actively embracing storytelling it might just get a little closer to the world it needs to reach. The main message of this book is that the *Business Story* needs to embrace the *Story Business* if it is to achieve its objectives.

But that's a snapshot of a stable landscape, which has persisted until relatively recently. Emerging developments mean this picture has to be revised and a new hypothesis proposed.

The three spheres can be understood historically as well as spatially. They correspond to three roughly sequential epochs, each with its own timeline. The timeline for the first sphere is the longest, stretching from prehistory up to the present day and beyond. The same impulse to tell, consume and share stories characterises this vast expanse of history. And whilst different technological and socio-economic developments have changed the way this fundamental impulse has been indulged in or exploited, the basic cognitive equipment within humans has remained exactly the same. Humankind is the universal variable in this timeline, which runs unbroken through all the developments associated with the other two spheres.

The second sphere is the second oldest, and its timeline starts some time at the origins of recorded history and literacy, where the oral traditions of narrative started to gain recognisable and reproducible shape. Archetypes and mythological figures that had circulated in oral forms, and associated with religious beliefs became literary figures whose adventures gave pleasure for their own sake. With Homer the figure of the poet as (semi) professional storyteller was born. Formal rules, such as those stipulated in Aristotle's *Poetics*, and subsequent arts of 'Poesie', ensured that storytelling was elevated into a craft dominated by a literate, leisured elite.

The two main strands that characterise this timeline are singleness of authority and the increasing distribution of content through successive technological developments. Whilst oral storytelling belonged to everyone, professional storytelling established the author as a single source of meaning and value. The most famous example of the multiple becoming singular is the editing and translation of the Bible into a closed and approved authority (the exact antithesis of the Wiki ethos).

With print the fluid became fixed and ownable. Poets, dramatists, novelists, and then film-makers put their stamp on ideas, by deftly wielding the formal tools of the craft. Post-Enlightenment, the poetic became the professional, and in time authors claimed intellectual property in their stories. Copyright became internationally established in the nineteenth century to allow authors to own and restrict the commercial reproduction of their stories that could now be circulated by print technology on a mass scale. From the printing press to the television, and then the Internet, technology has enabled authors to disseminate their stories to larger and larger audiences, as a way of exploiting the intellectual property residing in their words on a page or images on a screen. Authors ultimately became brands in this epoch.

## *Storytelling comes full circle*

But the Internet and social networking have started to shift the balance of power, and bring about something of a revolution in storytelling. A revolution because, by challenging the 'Broadcast' mode of single source authorship and controlled technological dissemination, storytelling is re-acquiring many of its earliest attributes. By forging ahead through technology, it is actually returning to its origins in some of the following ways:

**From authorial owners to multiple sharers.** Before writing and the rise of the professional author as the single source of content, stories belonged to everybody. They would circulate freely in different forms, evolving with each retelling into something new. In the oral tradition stories remained permanently work-in-progress and collectivist. Something of this ethos is returning with the distributive publishing of content across social networks.

Jonah Sachs has recently pointed to the paradox that digital technology is actually encouraging a return to oral traditions of pre-professional narrative participation. He uses the term 'Digitoral' to characterise this ironic quirk of history. For him Digitoral marks the demise of the Broadcast epoch dominated by the professional practices of the *Story Business*. As he explains, in the Broadcast tradition information is generated, fixed and disseminated by an elite, and so it's "very difficult, and usually illegal, to change it. Audiences don't interpret it, mash it up, and retell it… They consume it". In the Digitoral era, however, "ideas are never fixed: they're owned and modified by everyone. They move through networks at the will of their members and without that activity, they die". Distribution technologies have initiated a return to oral traditions, enabling the many to participate in and transform what was once controlled by the few.

YouTube perhaps provides the most mainstream manifestation of this ethos at work for pop culture, but it has made significant inroads into the very heartland of professional storytelling in the shape of Fan Fiction. The most powerful stories have always taken on lives of their own, growing in the imaginations of their audiences to achieve mythic existence beyond the confines of the page. Sites like Fanfiction.net allow the possibilities envisaged in the original cannon of writers such as J.K. Rowling, Stephanie Meyers, and even Conan Doyle or Dickens, to be explored through fictional elaboration by a community of creative devotees.

As the earliest fictions were myths and legends, with multiple variants about the exploits of mythical beings, so the most popular genres for technologically-enabled transformation reside in the fantasy end of the fictional spectrum. The most popular book-based canons to be given this fan-fuelled afterlife on Fanfiction.net are *Harry Potter*, *Twilight*, and *Lord of the Rings*. The mythic is as relevant and as resonant today as it was for pre-professional narrative communities. The impassioned involvement of industrious *amateurs* restores the positive meaning of that temporarily degraded term, as one laborious for the genuine love of it.

**From passive, private consumption to real-time active participation.** Stories were originally publically performed rather than privately consumed. Drama derived from religious rituals, and something of public performance of narrative survived even into the nineteenth-century. Before the rise of mass literacy and cheap paper, stories would be read aloud to large groups of individuals. The reading of stories at school, or by parents preserves some of this ritualistic magic. Children love (although parents hate) hearing the same story over and over again. Partly because they learn by repetition, and take pleasure in recognition of the familiar in the formative stages of cognitive development, but also because of the incantatory ritualistic nature of storytelling. Story is not entirely about content, part of its pleasure resides in the act of sharing the experience with others.

Whilst passive consumption of stories has characterised, at least the literary arts, since the Renaissance, something of the experiential aspect of communication has returned. The multiple connectedness of isolated individuals through technology, paradoxically brings them closer than they have been for decades. The real-time exchange of anecdotes, stories, and pre-eminently video as the viral medium of choice, around the globe makes narrative participatory again. Video is far more social than text, and its contagiousness as a medium underlines the appetite for the social aspects of narrative exchange *social* media has restored.

**Gossip goes global.** At the very least, the human need to communicate has gained unprecedented amplification and potential influence by the technologies at its disposal. I suggested that gossip is perhaps the most representative narrative mode of the *Story Impulse*. And it is gossip, in various shapes that keeps the Twitter feeds and word-of-mouth global grapevines so voluminously buzzing. As Peter Morville observes:

"Of course, we've co-opted the technology infrastructure, extended the locus of gossip from the water cooler to cyberspace... at the heart of many of today's killer applications lies the power and prevalence of gossip. It may not be ideal with respect to ethics or efficiency, but it's the way people are wired, and the blueprint is ancient and immutable".

In various ways the "ancient and immutable" impulses of story gain mastery of the media of its mass circulation. The oral, the collectivist and the anecdotal restore storytelling to its pre-professional origins. That is not to say that the identifiable forms and structures of the *Story Business* have been completely abandoned in this new world of empowered amateurs. These principles were formalised because they rested upon the psychological needs narrative has always served. From the very start, social media expressed an ingrained narrative bias and conformed to storytelling conventions.

The first popular incarnations of what is now called social media were memorial. Sites like classmates.com (1995-) and friendsreunited (2000-) in the UK allowed the 'back stories' of millions of lives to be revisited and resumed. These reconnections no doubt reignited countless old flames, and so 'up-dating' became literally that: updating 'what might have been' into 'happy ever after'. Romance and nostalgia turned a geeky coterie into a mainstream phenomenon, driven by the urge to connect through reminiscence. Friendsreunited has even spawned an offshoot called 'genesreunited' to allow the back stories of millions to take on generational dimensions. Preserving genealogy was one of the earliest functions of oral poetry, as all those tedious lists of ancestors in Norse sagas testify. Blogs revived the epistolary and diary forms of some of the earliest novels, where authors then and now wanted to bring dramatic immediacy and authentic intimacy to first-person accounts of the world in which they lived. Blogs live or die by the quality of their content and its ability to engage, adapting the rules of storytelling practice to the demands of concision in a highly competitive context.

And whilst social media is a living, performative form of expansive connectivity, it is leaving permanent traces that one day will render up meaningful narrative. Curatorial sites such as Pinterest constitute cabinets of online curiosities, living museums (and ultimately mausoleums) of our culture's enthusiasms. Facebook petrifies the events, likes and passing moods of all our yesterdays into public archives. We are now our own obituarists, curating and narrating our lives with their very passing.

Storytelling has undergone a revolution of access, but has not in itself fundamentally changed. What has changed is the ability of story consumers to become story creators and publishers, and for amateur gossipers to circulate their stories on a previously unimaginable scale. This is changing the profile of the story landscape as I've mapped it out. As the technologies and influence of what once belonged exclusively to the *Story Business* are used to fulfil the *Story Impulse* of millions, the borders of these two spheres are eroding and becoming increasingly blurred. The everyday world of non-professional, anecdotal exchange is in the ascendant. It is eclipsing in volume, and perhaps even influence, the products of professional storytellers and narrative influencers. If the first two spheres are merging, where does that leave the third and final sphere? How does this revolution in storytelling affect the *Business Story?*

## *The evolution of branding*

The timeline for the third sphere is the newest, and emerges in the period that witnessed the consolidation of intellectual property for authors and artists. The copyright phase of the *Story Business* overlaps with, and emerges from, the same commercial context that saw the birth of branding, and the stories that developed to promote this new phenomenon.

Brands emerged as symbols to identify goods, and stories accompanied these symbols in the form of advertising. These stories allowed ideas and emotions to be associated with these brands and thus enhance their value and promote their relevance to people's lives. Brands evolved from symbols into concepts. In time they became the sum of the ideas and perceptions (derived through experiences) that people formed about a product, service or organisation. Brands acquired meanings, and through these meanings articulated their relevance to people's lives.

Yet these explicit meanings were largely engineered by the marketers who dominated the media through which the ideas, emotions and stories associated with these brands were disseminated. The *Business Story*, like the *Story Business*, operated within the 'Broadcast' tradition, and relied on many of the same media of transmission. Declared brand meaning was primarily a one-way street, communicated through the marketing messages and narratives that gave shape to the ideas, emotions and experiences the brands were devised to convey.

Brands have always needed stories to convey their meanings. They have always generated stories too. As the most powerful works of fiction have given rise to countless sequels, offshoots and reincarnations, so the most iconic brands have generated more stories than they have told. Nike's 'Just do it' is the consummate consumer story generator. It is not the company's story, but the potential story of millions of individuals who respond to its clarion call. 'It' takes as many narrative shapes as the individual aspirations it reflects or inspires. It is not Nike's story, but a pre-existing myth the brand has made its own. The American Dream, no less, expressed in three monosyllables, and reinforced in a million stories of personal empowerment. Nike's own empowerment as a brand and a company is fuelled by these stories.

Yet, before the web and the social web, the impact and visibility of such stories were limited. They resided in the imaginations or memories of individuals, whilst anecdote or advocacy was confined to immediate word-of-mouth grapevines, and destined to die out as oral or personal ephemera. With this access revolution in storytelling, the oral becomes viral, and the personal becomes public and permanent. Instead of brands using stories to convey their meanings, stories are determining the meanings of brands. Brands are becoming the sum of the anecdotes circulated about them. And as there are more consumers out there than brands, campaigns or company-endorsed messages, there are potentially more consumer-generated stories circulating about a brand than those officially endorsed by its owner. If an anecdote can found a brand's story – a foundation myth, a moment of truth – then, through the amplification of social media, it can re-make or break it too. Brand has always been what people say it is; now those people have a much bigger and more impactful say.

Instead of customers passively consuming messages and actively purchasing goods or services, they can actively create and circulate their own stories. This has much more potential influence on a brand's fortunes than the official story. Brands came into their own during the industrial epoch in response to problems created by mass urbanisation. In the vast sprawling cities, no one knew whom to trust when purchasing goods or services. Compared with life in villages, there was little visibility, memory, relationship, gossip to enforce accountability, and so little trust. Brands stepped in to fulfil these needs.

Yet mass connectivity potentially makes the whole world a village again. We gather round the virtual global marketplace, conversations flow, relationships are built. Everything is visible, everything is traceable, everyone is accountable because gossip reigns supreme. We know whom to trust: our networks. The problem that branding emerged to solve is therefore no longer so urgently apparent. As long as there is competition there will be a need for branding; yet the concept has to evolve if it is to remain relevant to audiences who can now participate in the creation and circulation of meaning. Storytelling can provide the solution, but storytelling adapted to the new landscape of empowered co-creative participation.

# *The evolution of corporate storytelling?*

A high-profile example of this happening is Coca-Cola's content marketing manifesto, 'Liquid and Linked', launched in April 2011. Coke calculated that only ten percent of the content about its brands on popular sites such as YouTube was actually produced by the company. Coke's response was to start actively engaging such users as co-creative partners in its story. The company describes this move as: "a big step in the way we interact with consumers ... moving from one-way messages… to creating engaging experiences and back-and-forth dialogue" about its brands. For as they concede: "no one has the smarts on ideas". So they are now listening to consumer ideas and input, and involving them as participants in the meanings of their brands. "Liquid and Linked ideas must provoke conversations and then The Coca-Cola Company must react to those conversations 365 days a year". This dynamic approach signals what Coke sees as the "evolution of storytelling" for the company. The global Goliath of brand promotion starts to put its Broadcast days behind it.

It makes a lot of sense for consumer brands to go with the narrative flow. Brands have always craved meaning, and need to maintain their relevance. Here is the means to achieve both, combining viral advocacy and market testing in one fell swoop. Indeed, Coke refers to market data as the "the new soil in which our ideas will grow, and data whisperers will become the new messiahs".

Yet, this is actually The Coca-Cola Company talking here. Its new manifesto is designed to involve all its stakeholders from consumers to investors in the telling of its story. A bold corporate ambition is behind these changes. As it declares: "The Coca-Cola Company intends to double the size of the business between now and 2020 and so that means that every single marketing norm needs to be reconsidered if we're going to meet such aggressive volume and business growth objectives". 'Liquid and Linked' is the result of this radical rethink, and sees the company moving from being about "creative excellence to content excellence". Or, from a producer and promoter of world-dominating brands to a circulator of stories.

A major step in this direction was taken in November 2012 (just as I thought I was finishing this book), with the complete reinvention of Coca-Cola's corporate website, as an interactive magazine. Whilst retaining the same url – *http://www.coca-colacompany.com/* – the site has been rebranded as Coca-Cola Journey (what else?), and launched as a story-sharing hub for the company and its brands.

Story is everywhere you look on Journey. It is the first item on the primary navigation, where 'About us' is usually found, and is the dominant focus of a homepage that is continually refreshed with new rich content. Instead of the hero shots broadcasting corporate messages, they instead share stories through video, blogs or social media feeds. Coca-Cola is still very much the star of the show. But then, Journey was originally an internal magazine, reinvented as the company's principal corporate communications hub. As a spokesman explains: "We had brand pages, but there was nothing that knitted it all together into the story of us… So we wanted to take all that great storytelling that we were sharing internally and share it with the world."

Coke has a lot of history and vast operations, and so there is a lot of Coke content to share around. Whilst the content is Coke themed, it's anything but dry corporate monologue. There are Coke-themed recipes; innovation videos about bottling materials told from a human perspective; archive memorabilia; Sustainability stories about what Coke calls its 'community' around the world; investor information and 'Business' stories and opinions; and people features drawn from its 700,000 plus employee base. Coke has a lot to say, but it also has over 50 million Facebook fans, and is actively engaging with them and other social media communities to involve them in the Journey. There are imbedded customised social media feeds throughout, systematic cross-pollination of content across the main social media sites, and a coordinated effort to encourage inbound traffic to its story-sharing hub. Inbound and outbound, everything is brought together through storytelling.

This is what 'Liquid and Linked' is all about. 'Liquid' is about circulation of content. If the content isn't compelling enough no one is going to share it. And if they can't tell their story on the most basic mobile phone, then, in the words of a Coke spokeswoman, "we haven't finished telling our story". Which is where 'Linked' comes in. Whilst its content needs to circulate freely, this content must flow from and back to a clear brand strategy and a coherent idea. That idea is 'Open Happiness', the latest iteration of Coke's consumer strapline, and the single-minded focus of their new content marketing crusade. As Coke explains: "The role of Content Excellence is to behave like a ruthless editor otherwise we'll risk just creating noise." Coca-Cola is thus applying the same 'ruthless' efficiency that has always characterised its brand management to its new incarnation as global storyteller.

Everything joins up, and everyone joins in, invited to be part of the Journey. This is not just a consumer brand paying lip service to an empowered demographic it wants to target. Not just. This is one of the world's biggest companies throwing open its principal corporate communication channel to involve all its audiences in the same story. Coke has multiple stakeholders and audiences, yet Journey makes little attempt to segregate them along approved corporate lines.

Investors rub shoulders with brand fans as part of a single community. Should the latter stray into the investor section they might encounter the following compliance jargon – "The following presentation may include certain 'non-GAAP financial measures' as defined in Regulation G under the Securities Exchange Act of 1934". Not much happiness there. Or should they discover that the company's declared vision is summed up in a single word – that isn't 'Happiness', but 'Profit' – they might briefly pause for thought. But on the other side of the coin, the investment community is given a clear demonstration of the value and currency of consistent storytelling. An ambitious growth target demands a single-minded narrative strategy. Yet Coke knows that storytelling is *the* universal human imperative: "at the heart of all families, communities and cultures and it's something that The Coca-Cola Company has excelled at for 125 years". And therefore in this new age of global conversations, narrative provides the best way to realise Coke's long cherished dream of being a universal currency. Teaching the world to sing its story through the channels of empowered amplification.

## *Only connect*

Coke's evolution into a storyteller perhaps marks a more significant evolution still: the evolution of branding from being about managing assets to sharing stories. This, I believe, is what's happening, and why the age-old arts of storytelling are newly relevant and urgently required. Even here, finally in the most resistant corner of the *Business Story* sphere: corporate communications. The corporate brand, like its consumer counterpart, must evolve if it is to remain relevant to those upon whom it ultimately depends. It must evolve into a storyteller.

Consumer brands have traditionally thrived through storytelling, creating works of narrative art in the form of advertising. The empowerment of users and audiences has compelled them to momentarily pause in their relentless monologue, and start listening... before rejoining what is now a conversation. As one content curation pundit perfectly summed it up, "When it comes to social content, you have to be more interesting than your audiences' friends". The brands that seek to start conversations have to be prepared to listen and respond to them too. Even the most interesting interruption is still an interruption if it doesn't allow co-creative input to define a brand's meaning and sharing its story.

Consumer brands have been searching for meaning for a long time. At first they needed to be merely preferred. Then they needed to be loved. Now they need to be shared. But brands are largely abstractions, made meaningful and tangible through experience. Experience leads to anecdote and through anecdote, advocacy. Sharing brand stories ultimately gives the brands the meaning they have always craved. Brings them to life, proves their relevance, gives them a voice. Product brands do not actually have voices (despite the infantalist babble of Innocent wannabes). But consumers do, and it's right that they should have a major say in the brand's meaning. A product brand can ultimately be what consumers say it is, and lose none of its identify or relevance. Quite the opposite. If the meanings it generates are positive and lead to advocacy then the brand has served its purpose. Like the best stories, it provides a mirror, reflecting the needs and desires of those with whom it interacts.

In this model, products and their promotion are no longer an industrial pipeline. But rather a grapevine, to be cultivated, harvested and showcased as living testimony to their relevance to consumers. The proof of the product is in the narratives that blossom around it. In this brave new world, stories do not so much promote brands, as provide vehicles for their meaning. If a product generates a lot of positive stories, then it is the proof of its relevance and resonance. These stories become part of the brand's own story. No longer abstractions associated with artificial needs, but the authentic, organic meanings expressed through the stories they give rise to. By entering into co-creative conversation, consumer brands future-proof their relevance for the networked generations.

If consumer brands need to listen, corporate brands need to talk. Whilst a product doesn't actually have a voice, a company does. And it needs to find it and use this far more effectively: by telling its story.

What the corporate world needs most, story does best: establish the human connections upon which trust is built. That doesn't mean every brand must or can afford to become a 'publisher' as many are now claiming. So much as being absolutely clear on what its core story has to say, and why this ultimately matters. Whilst consumer brands can be mercurially adaptive to the flow of conversations, the corporate brand needs to be far more focused, single-minded and, above all, articulate in the way it tells its story. Without a product, there are only relationships and experiences, and these can best be nurtured and expressed through narrative. The corporate brand has to adopt the role of storyteller if it is to fulfil its function where it is most needed. In fact, there has never been a greater need for the corporate brand, and a greater opportunity to serve its purpose through storytelling.

If a company doesn't tell its story there are likely to be plenty of others who will. This may not be quite the story the company wants to share; but if it has more clarity, volume and visibility than the messages the company itself sends, then this will stand for its story. Silence is not an option in this connected world of clamorous chatter. It only exacerbates mistrust, and ultimately isolation. A company has to put its story out there with clarity and conviction. It has to start the conversation with an articulate proposition, and ensure this holds up coherently, and flows consistently through all the channels of engagement.

If the core brand story is an authentic reflection of who it truly is, then the stories this gives rise to, the connections this makes, should be honest reflections too. A positive feedback loop will be established, endorsing and amplifying the narrative the company seeks to share. If the story needs to evolve, then so be it. It has to go out there and live in the imaginations and advocacy of those with whom it needs to connect. If it is flatly rejected, then this probably indicates that there is no substance to it. Then it must be rethought and redefined. The days of monologue are over.

As long as there is competition there will be a need for brands. Differentiation is still required. But this differentiation will be built on the meaningfulness of relationships. And this relationship will be truly that: a dynamic, mutually-beneficial connection, where all sides relate to and with the meaning of the brand. Brand may no longer be a thing, but a process. A verb more than a noun. A journey, experienced as story.

A shared story is not just something that connects with people, it is the connection – the trace of the brand's relevance, the narrative testament to its value and its truth. Corporate identity can live up to its name if it finds a human voice, a coherent sense of self, and an articulate, engaging expression of that self through the stories it shares. In this way story ultimately fulfils the promise of brand. It connects rationally, because there will be a clear integrity of idea and its expression; and emotionally, because the defined need it serves will get to the very core of what it means to be human. Story is *the* universal human connector.

A connected world demands a connected currency. Story has always played this role. Its true domain is the imagination, its true vehicle is the flow and exchange of ideas, circulating and surviving as a currency with the power to change how people think, feel and act. Ultimately a power to change the world. Stories were 'viral' before the metaphor became a buzzword. The conditions are now right for an epidemic of narrative. The Internet and social web are simply testimony to the human urge to narrative, to make connections through the currency of human relationships that is storytelling.

The *Story Impulse* is as strong as it has ever been, and can now be expressed through the means and media that once belonged exclusively to the *Story Business*. As these two spheres merge into one, there is one natural course for the corporate world to take – and that is to connect with the world of human beings through storytelling. As spheres one and two increasingly converge, becoming a universal zone of empowered, connected narrative, story is set to conquer its final frontier: the corporate world. Business must now connect with the world upon which it ultimately depends. Then there will be one sphere, one world, brought together through storytelling.

There really only is one world. Live in fragments no longer. Only connect.

THE STORYSHIP
ENTERPRISE

# Notes and Bibliographic References

——

## *Preface*

Paul Smith, *Lead With A Story: A Guide to Crafting Business Narratives That Captivate, Convince, and Inspire* (AMACOM, 2012).

Robert McKee, *Story: Substance, Structure, Style and Principles of Screenwriting* (Methuen, 1999). This is an extraordinarily readable and humbling book, which deserves its status as the definitive guide to the craft. Erudite, expert and thorough, it presents the principles and pitfalls of storytelling in a clear and engaging way.

## *The Beginning*

### *Why Story*

The 'interpreter' was discovered by a neuroscientist called Michael Gazzaniga, whose work is summarised in Jonathan Gottschall's excellent book, *The Storytelling Animal: How Stories Make Us Human* (Houghton Mifflin, 2012). This book explores a number of hypotheses about why humans need to tell stories, and whilst it doesn't quite identify a definitive answer, it's a fascinating and thought-provoking survey. Gottschall also usefully summarises the idea that fiction works as a flight simulator for the brain: "The constant firing of our neurons in response to fictional stimuli strengthens and refines the neural pathways that lead to the skilful navigation of life's problems... Fiction allows our brains to practice reacting to the kinds of challenges that are, and always were, most crucial to our success as a species".

On the history of brands and branding, see Wally Olins', *On Brand* (Thames & Hudson, 2004); *Corporate Identity* (Thames & Hudson, 1989).

2012 was definitely the year story came to prominence as a business tool. It saw the publication of Paul Smith's *Lead With a Story* as well as Jonah Sach's *Winning the Story Wars* (Harvard Business Press, 2012). Sachs' polemical *tour de force* is particularly compelling, also comprising a lot of what I stress about the instinctive and archetypal power of narrative persuasively applied to a marketing context. His emphasis on marketers as the modern mythmakers conclusively argues for the need to apply mythic thinking to communications. His observations about how social networking is returning storytelling back to its pre-professional, oral foundations, chimes exactly with my own argument developed at the end of my book. His term for this development as the 'digitoral' era neatly sums up the paradox I was blindly groping to articulate. Sachs is on a messianic marketing mission in his book, claiming that marketing needs to reinvent itself through storytelling. Going from the old model of trading on people's inadequacies to empowering consumers and citizens to find the possibility of fulfilment in the morals marketing stories can present. It's a thrilling, insightful journey he takes us on.

Paul Smith's book, referenced earlier, is a useful addition to what might be termed the 'Leadership Fables' genre of business book. How-to instruction manuals in the narrative art of persuasion. This is most famously exemplified by Stephen Denning's pioneering work *The Springboard: How Storytelling Ignites Action in Knowledge-Era Organizations* from 2000. This provided business leaders with alternatives to the more analytical methods they had traditionally employed when seeking to influence behaviour. Instead of giving people facts and figures, and reasons to do something, Smith and Denning suggest using an anecdote or a parable to bring the idea to life. Smith's book even features "powerful stories for 21 of the toughest challenges business people face". Whilst some of the methods and insights are relevant to my chapter on Employee Engagement, my emphasis is less on storytelling as an internal leadership tool, so much as an external communications one. Annette Simmons' *The Story Factor: Inspiration, Influence and Persuasion Through the Art of Storytelling* (Basic Books, 2006), is another essential guide to using story to influence, both inside and outside of the business context. It delves deep into the humanity and psychology of storytelling in all contexts, not just to 'Win', or 'Lead' in the business jungle. I found Simmons' book invaluable for understanding the human dynamics of narrative.

John Simmons is the author of *Innocent*, which was originally in the Great Brand Stories series, now published by Marshall Cavendish (revised edition, 2011). He is most famously the author of *Me, We, Them and It* (2002); *Dark Angels* (2004); and *The Invisible Grail* (2006), collected as *TheWriter™ Trilogy* and now also published by Marshall Cavendish. He also edited a collection of essays called *Bard & Co: Shakespeare's Role in Modern Business* (2007), to which I contributed a humble chapter on what *Timon of Athens* might teach us about financial crisis. Simmons is clearly not afraid of mentioning Shakespeare in a boardroom.

## What Makes a Story

Brand "the most valuable real estate in the world", quoted by John Hegarty in *Hegarty on Advertising: Turning Intelligence into Magic* (Thames & Hudson, 2011).

Emotional connection is an unavoidable function of our cognitive life as primates. Brian Boyd refers to an "emotional contagion" that takes place instinctively when normal brains are shown representations of emotions. He refers to something called "mirror neurons … [which] fire when we see others act or express emotion as if we were making the same action, and allow us through a kind of automatic inner imitation to understand their intentions and attune ourselves to their feelings". This is the basis of empathy in art, allowing us to relate closely with fictional characters in the way we would with real humans. We just can't help tuning in to others' emotions, something that confers vital educative functions in social units, and allows us to 'read' people as indexes to survival. That is why trust is fundamentally an emotional value, and has little to do with the rational arguments we might offer. Brian Boyd's illuminating and persuasive book, *On the Origin of Stories: Evolution, Cognition, and Fiction* (Harvard

University Press, 2009) informed many of the points I make about the human bias towards storytelling.

Apart from the works referenced, I found the following books useful in writing this chapter:

Aristotle, *The Poetics*, translated S. H. Butcher (Kindle edn.)

Brooker, Christopher, *The Seven Basic Plots: Why We Tell Stories* (Continuum, 2005)

Forster, E. M., *Aspects of the Novel*, edited Oliver Stallybrass (Penguin, 2005)

Frye, Northrop, *An Anatomy of Criticism: Four Essays* (Princeton UP., 1992)

Goleman, Daniel, *Emotional Intelligence: Why it Can Matter More than IQ* (Bloomsbury, 1996)

*Heath, Chip and Dan, Made to Stick: Why Some Ideas Take Hold and Others Come Unstuck* (Arrow, 2008)

Wood, James, *How Fiction Works* (Vintage, 2009)

# The Middle

## How to Develop your Story

The classic work on the archetypal hero's quest is Joseph Campbell's, *The Hero with a Thousand Faces* (1949), which famously inspired George Lucas in writing *Star Wars*. This is available in an updated re-print of 2004, published by Princeton University Press, from which my quotation comes.

The application of Jungian psychology to branding is developed by Margaret Mack and Carol S Pearson in *The Hero and the Outlaw: Building Extraordinary Brands Through the Power of Archetypes* (McGraw Hill, 2001). Jonah Sachs offers a succinct application of Campbell's classic Hero's Journey story structure in his *Winning the Story Wars*, to help marketers think about their brand's type, and thus the key to their story.

"Don't give audiences 4, give them 2 + 2", Andrew Stanton, in a TED talk on storytelling. There are some excellent insights, and what endeared me to Mr Stanton most of all, is his starting his talk with one of my all time favourite jokes about a man and a goat. *http://www.youtube.com/watch?v=KxDwieKpawg* (Accessed August 2012).

## Where to Tell your Story

### Through Annual Reporting

'Rising to the Challenge' is available at: *http://www.frc.org.uk/Our-Work/Publications/ASB/Rising-to-the-Challenge/Rising-to-the-challenge.aspx* (Accessed August 2012).

### Through your People

The role of storytelling for engaging employees is well established in the literature. Annette Simmons' *The Story Factor* proposes numerous ways in which the psychology of narrative can help influence people to act differently in diverse organisational settings. Similarly, most of the scenarios and narrative formulas outlined in Stephen Denning's *Leader's Guide to Storytelling* use stories to help managers address specific people issues within organisations. Denning outlines a whole variety of different story genres designed to meet these specific challenges. His most famous genre 'The Springboard Story', for example, is useful for leaders who need to effect change, but are likely to meet resistance. Instead of just telling people what they need to do or ought to do, you find an appropriate anecdote to inspire people to imagine and feel the advantages of embracing change. Story provides a springboard into a new reality far more effectively than presenting a rational case for change. Story for both these writers is a people-focused tool, that comes into its element less through communications channels than through direct personal and collective engagements. Readers seeking practical guidance for specific scenarios would do well to consult these books.

Wally Olins, *On Brand* (Thames & Hudson, 2004).

## *Through the Digital Universe*

On standing out through the use of moving image, see *http://www.globalspeak.com/component/content/article/47-promo/126-online-video-benefits-.html*
An updated version of the Forbes Insights research is found at: *http://images.forbes.com/forbesinsights/StudyPDFs/Video_in_the_CSuite.pdf*

Both sources were accessed December 2012.

*The Cluetrain Manifesto: The End of Business as Usual*, was published in April 1999 by Christopher Locke, David Weinberger, Rick Levine, and David Searls. The core idea that the Internet that attempted to market to people in bland business speak, and the Internet of 'market' conversations would one day converge appears to be happening. The main message that business needs to speak in a human voice and be part of planet earth is relevant still. The train has a few more stops to go. For the purposes of this chapter I used the ten-year anniversary edition of the Manifesto, published by Basic Books in 2011.

Charlene Li and Josh Bernoff, *Marketing in the Groundswell* (Harvard Business Press, 2009).

# The End?

## Where Story is going

Peter Morville, *Ambient Findability: What We Find Changes Who We Become* (O'Reilly, 2005).

The best way to get to grips with Liquid and Linked is the explanatory video the company posted on YouTube. *http://www.youtube.com/ watch?v=LerdMmWjU_E*

This is an animated narration of the new policy by Jonathan Mildenhall, the VP, Global Advertising Strategy and Content Excellence at The Coca-Cola Company. You see Coke takes this seriously, his title was VP of 'Creative Excellence' until recently. A transcript of a talk given by Mildenhall explaining the new policy in April 2012 is available at: *http://www.my-mip.com/RM/RM_ MIPWORLD/2012/documents/pdf/transcripts/miptv-2012-media- mastermind-keynote-jonathan-mildenhall-transcript.pdf*

Quotations about 'Liquid and Linked' are taken from the video or transcript.

All quotations about Coca-Cola Journey are from Ashley Brown, Coke's director of digital communications and social media, quoted from the site itself: *http://www.coca-colacompany.com/media-center/ press-releases/coca-cola-invites-the-world-to-join-its-new-journey* or in a *New York Times article that broke the story: http://www.nytimes. com/2012/11/12/business/media/coke-revamps-web-site-to-tell-its- story.html?ref=business&_r=0.*

See also *http://www.brandchannel.com/home/post/2012/11/12/Coca- Cola-Storytelling-Digital-Journey-111212.aspx*

The Coke spokeswoman on the need for the company to tell its story on even a simple mobile phone is Wendy Clark head of integrated marketing and communications, speaking at an *Ad Age* Digital Conference, in April 2012. A video of her talk is at *http://adage.*

*com/article/special-report-digital-conference/coca-cola-s-wendy-clark-liquid-linked-key/226836/*

"Be more interesting than your audience's friends" came from Noah Brier of Percolate in an *Internet Week* panel on how 2012 was "the Year Social Helps Brands Become Publishers", a YouTube video of the panel held in May 2012 is found at:

*http://www.youtube.com/watch?v=ihr77Xaip6Y*

All online sources for this chapter were accessed December 2012.

In addition to the works cited, I found the following books useful in writing this chapter:

Anderson, Chris, *The Longer Long Tail: How Endless Choice is Creating Unlimited Demand* (Random House, Business; 2009)

Briggs, Asa and Burke, Peter, *A Social History of the Media: From Gutenberg to the Internet* (Polity, 2010)

Godin, Seth, *Tribes: We Need You to Lead Us* (Piatkus, 2008)

Millman, Debbie, *Brand Thinking and Other Noble Pursuits* (Allworth Press, 2011)

Walker, Rob, *I'm With the Brand The Secret Dialogue Between What We Buy and Who We Are* (Constable, 2008)

# Acknowledgements

—

First, I'd like to thank Martin Liu at LID Publishing for suggesting the book. Then I'd like to thank all the people who contributed to, designed up or delivered this book. This means: Isabel, Brett, Dean, Martin and Ben for their insights; Jim Bodoh, Andrew Gorman and Andrew Doyle for their comments and suggestions; Damo, Nick, Jevon and Henry for visual magic; Dean Radley, David Williams, David King, Michelle Obee, and Priti Kochhar for making it happen. Most of all, I'd like to thank Carl Radley for supporting the project, and encouraging its fruition (not to mention allowing me to flit off to Spain). The big heart at the centre of a great company. Thanks to the Madrid gang for terraza support, Dan King, Matt Atchison, and Ian Newman. Finalmente, muchas gracias Miren, por todo.

**Declaration:** somewhere I have a few shares in Pearson from my days at Penguin, but that's not why I said nice things about their annual report.

**Credits:** designed by Nicholas May, Jevon Downer and Damian Nowell. Illustrations: Jevon Downer. Author photo: Henry Thomas.

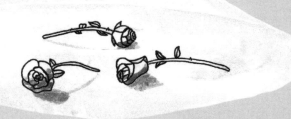

# *About the author*

Robert Mighall has had quite a varied career up to now, but the common thread running through his biography is 'story'.

He has a PhD in English Literature and History, and once held a research fellowship at Merton College, University of Oxford, where he wrote a book on Victorian fiction.

After Oxford he went on to be the editor of the Penguin Classics series, where he was responsible for ensuring the world's greatest stories were made available and accessible for modern readers. He has published and lectured on the likes of Oscar Wilde, Charles Dickens, Robert Louis Stevenson, William Shakespeare, John Keats, and William Butler Yeats.

From looking after a famous brand, he went agency side to create them. He is now a writer/brand-consultant/corporate-storyteller for London-based design and communications agency Radley Yeldar, the largest independent integrated communications business in Europe.

His role is to discover the big ideas behind brands, and give them clear and coherent expression across a range of corporate communications. His clients include GSK, Shell, Lloyds Banking Group, Anglo American, Steria and Pearson.

*Only Connect* draws on insights from both sides of Robert's professional experience, connecting what he learnt from the Story Business to the development of Business Stories. Eroding distinctions between these two worlds through the principles of effective storytelling is what this, his first business book, is all about.

# BEYOND
## THE WRITTEN WORD

### Authors who speak to you face to face.

Discover LID Speakers, a service
that enables businesses to have
direct and interactive contact with
the best ideas brought to their
own sector by the most
outstanding creators
of business thinking.

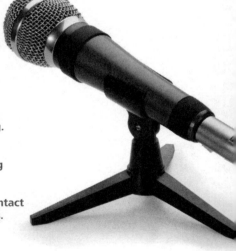

- A network specialising in business
  speakers, making it easy to find the
  most suitable candidates.

- A website with full details and videos,
  so you know exactly who you're hiring.

- A forum packed with ideas and
  suggestions about the most interesting
  and cutting-edge issues.

- A place where you can make direct contact
  with the best in international speakers.

- The only speakers' bureau backed up
  by the expertise of an established
  business book publisher.

LIDspeakers
.com

Sure value.